THE SAVINGS AND LOAN CRISIS

THE SAVINGS
AND LOAN CRISIS

An Annotated Bibliography

Compiled by
Pat L. Talley

Bibliographies and Indexes in Economics and Economic History,
Number 14

Greenwood Press
Westport, Connecticut • London

Library of Congress Cataloging-in-Publication Data

Talley, Pat L.
   The savings and loan crisis : an annotated bibliography / compiled
by Pat L. Talley.
      p.   cm.—(Bibliographies and indexes in economics and
economic history, ISSN 0749-1786 ; no. 14)
   Includes index.
   ISBN 0-313-28833-X (alk. paper)
   1. Savings and loan association failures—United States—
Bibliography.   2. Savings and loan associations—United States—
Bibliography.   3. Savings and Loan Bailout, 1989—Bibliography.
I. Title. II. Series.
Z7164.F5T23   1993
[HG2151]
016.3323'2'0973—dc20   93-12910

British Library Cataloguing in Publication Data is available.

Library of Congress Catalog Card Number: 93-12910
ISBN: 0-313-28833-X
ISSN: 0749-1786

First published in 1993

Greenwood Press, 88 Post Road West, Westport, CT 06881
An imprint of Greenwood Publishing Group, Inc.

Printed in the United States of America

The paper used in this book complies with the
Permanent Paper Standard issued by the National
Information Standards Organization (Z39.48-1984).

10 9 8 7 6 5 4 3 2 1

Affectionately dedicated
to my daughter Desel and to my Dad.

*It is dearness only that gives
everything its value.*
Thomas Paine

CONTENTS

ACKNOWLEDGMENTS

The support of my colleagues has made this volume possible. I owe thanks to many for sharing materials with me, and for providing encouragement. The staff of the Irving Public Library showed the greatest patience with my requests for Interlibrary Loan materials. Special thanks to James Karney, John LaRoche, and Theresa Woods. Appreciation is due also to libraries that are willing to share their collections through ILL. Librarian colleagues who shared materials directly from their libraries were: John Adams, Hopkins & Sutter, Dallas; Carolyn Grimes, Locke Purnell Rain Harrell, Dallas; Inga Govaars, Federal Home Loan Bank of San Francisco; Kit Harahan, Savings & Community Bankers of America, Washington, D.C.; Juliette Levinton, Federal Home Loan Bank of New York; Anita Lublink, Federal Home Loan Bank of Atlanta; Sue Ridnour and Mary Ann Wacker, Haynes & Boone, Dallas; Nola Sterling and Diana Parker, Federal Home Loan Bank of Seattle; Karen Marie Williams, Hogan & Hartson, Washington, D.C.; Cheryl Wright, Office of Thrift Supervision, Washington, D.C.; and Mike Zimmerman, Federal Reserve Bank of Dallas. My heartfelt thanks to all! My daughter, Desel Hair, conducted database searches, offered encouragement, and listened to my concerns. I am very grateful for her support. My friend, Sue Haarala, was kind enough to proofread the text, which was an invaluable help to me. I also appreciate the work of Kathryn Thomas whose word processing expertise was especially helpful.

I would like to express my gratitude to the management of the Federal Home Loan Bank of Dallas for their strong support of the bank's library. I appreciate the opportunity I have had to grow professionally since establishing the Research and Information Library in 1983. I have been fortunate to have worked with very supportive supervisors through the years. I am grateful to Tom Hendricks for his vision. My warmest thanks go to Karen Krug whose encouragement was invaluable. The success of the library is due to the wonderful staff with whom I have worked. Each person's contribution is deeply appreciated. Laurie Ingraham and Adrienne Spratt were there during the "crazy" years; thanks for all of the hard work and friendship. I have had the pleasure of working with Nancy Garza for the past four years, and I value her as a co-worker, and a friend.

INTRODUCTION

PURPOSE

Countless books and articles have been written on the savings and loan crisis. I rather suspect that the massive amount of information on the topic is what prompts the queries I receive as a reference librarian. The caller is generally seeking the definitive title on this topic. A recommendation of one or two titles across the board is not feasible. Although many inclusive titles have been written, great care must be taken in looking at the publication date, focus of the information, and the author's background or affiliation. Additionally, the needs of the researcher must be considered. Questions come from law firms involved in litigation as well as students from high school through post graduate studies. Each of the users requires different materials to meet his needs. The impetus to compile this bibliography evolved from the various needs of researchers which have been brought to my attention as librarian of the Federal Home Loan Bank of Dallas. The purpose of this bibliography is to help locate titles which address specific aspects of the savings and loan crisis. It is hoped that the annotations provided will reduce research time by eliminating the need to search through many titles to find the required subject information.

SCOPE

The titles included in the bibliography are those published between 1980-1992. The topics are related to the savings and loan crisis, or by extension to S&L viability or profitability. The terms "thrift" and "savings and loan" are used interchangeably throughout the text. It is very important to note the publication date when considering the usefulness of a title. Annotations were written from the viewpoint of the information presented. However, from our current perspective, the information especially "facts & figures," must be considered in light of the time in which it was written. In addition to noting the scope of the information provided in each title, the author's industry affiliation is often reflected. When the author's affiliation is of interest it is noted in at least one annotation. The author's stand on the issues is illuminating. It is important to note the authors, many of whom are economists, whose opinions have been expressed from as early as the late 1970s through the current literature. It is interesting to trace their thoughts related to the savings and loan industry as the crisis evolved. Other authors write from the perspective of their affiliation with industry, consumer, or media groups. These affiliations should be taken into consideration when studying the material presented.

SOURCES

The titles included in the bibliography are primarily books and research papers. They cover the gamut from scholarly works to "exposes" or "popular" books. The titles were gathered from references in book and paper bibliographies, reviews, articles, online database searches, and library collections. The goal of the bibliography is to be as inclusive as possible. The inclusiveness was limited by the materials which were identified but could not be located through Interlibrary Loan, or through other contacts. Journal articles are not included in this bibliography as numerous indexes cover this information. Please see the section titled "Other Sources of Information" at the end of this introduction for suggestions on broadening one's research on the topic. Congressional hearings, testimony, and General Accounting Office publications are not included. Citations to these publications are easily found through the **Monthly Catalog of United States Government Publications**. This is the print version of the **Catalog** which lists reports, studies, and conference proceedings issued by all U.S. federal government agencies and the U.S. Congress. The equivalent, the **GPO Monthly Catalog**, is available through private databases and on CD-Rom. The coverage is from July 1976 to the present, and includes all Senate and House hearings on private and public bills and laws. Although the **GPO Monthly Catalog** is available on several databases, the one most readily available to the general public is **First Search**. Many universities and public libraries allow public access to **First Search**. Fees for this service vary. **First Search** is accessible from the **OCLC Online Union Catalog** and through **Internet** as a gateway. Government depository libraries should serve as the starting point for access to these publications. The extent of the collection available varies with the depository. A list of depositories should be available at any public library. **A Directory of U.S. Government Depository Libraries** may be ordered from the U.S. Government Printing Office. Another index to Congressional publications available both in hard copy and on CD-Rom is the **Congressional Information Service Index**. This title indexes House, Senate, and joint committee and subcommittee publications. Included are committee hearings and prints, reports, documents, and special publications. This index is usually available at large public libraries and universities. Dissertations were included in this collection only if the title or author is of particular note. The crisis has become a popular dissertation topic. Access to a listing of dissertations is available as **Dissertations Abstracts Online**. The hard copy versions are **American Doctoral Dissertations** and **Dissertation Abstracts International**.

ARRANGEMENT OF ENTRIES

The entries in this book are arranged by subject. Background or history of savings and loans is contained to some extent in the majority of the titles. Information presented in the titles may overlap in other areas as well. The title was placed within the subject to which it makes the largest contribution for our purposes. The chapters are arranged in chronological order where possible beginning with the "Depository Institutions Deregulation and Monetary Control Act" of 1980. The entries are arranged alphabetically by author's last name, or by title if no author's name is given. For multiple entries by the same author, the titles written by the author alone are listed first. Works edited by the author follow, with those coauthored listed last. The chapter entitled "Thrift Industry" is divided into subchapters by publication date, and alphabetically within that breakdown. It is possible to trace the evolution of the crisis by approaching the material in this manner. A brief discussion of some of the chapters is presented below.

CHAPTER OVERVIEW

A review of the industry literature shows that the "savings and loan crisis" did not begin in the 1980s. Some authors trace it to the 1960s, some to 1979, while others state that it began when the Federal Home Loan Bank System was created in 1932. Many suggest that the structure of the System doomed it to failure. Two acts, the DIDMCA (1980) and Garn-St Germain (1982) were written to try to solve problems which existed at the time. Garn-St Germain was signed on October 15, 1982 by President Reagan. It was enacted to help thrifts respond to the high interest rate environment. The role these acts played in the crisis are fully explored by the titles included in this bibliography. It is interesting to note that new real estate lending guidelines adopted in October 1992 are the same limits which were in effect until repealed by Garn-St Germain.

It is not possible to consider the thrift crisis without examining deposit insurance. The titles included in this chapter relate to the thrift industry in some manner. Titles specific to commercial banking were not included. The deposit insurance reform "debate" still continues. A first step has been taken toward reform with the implementation of a transitional risk-based premium system on January 1, 1993. A more permanent system is scheduled to take effect January 1, 1994. Many of the economists quoted in this bibliography are still urging changes to the fundamental structure of the deposit insurance system. Uncertainty exists concerning the Savings Association Insurance Fund (SAIF). The late William Taylor, the former Federal Deposit Insurance Corporation chairman, testified in July 1992 that the fund might not be adequately funded by its start date in October 1993 to exercise resolution authority for future thrift failures.

The future of the thrift industry is still widely debated, with a broad range of opinions expressed. Additional funding for the Resolution Trust Corporation has not been forthcoming. The "S&L Debacle" was "discussed" at the 1992 Democratic Convention in speeches made by New York Governor Mario Cuomo and Jesse Jackson. Robert Reischauer, Director of the Congressional Budget Office, presented his view of thrifts in the year 2000 in testimony before the Senate Banking Committee. He foresees a concentration in real estate finance, while continuing to provide depository and lending services. The Federal Home Loan Bank System is changing to meet the guidelines established for it by the Financial Institutions Reform, Recovery, and Enforcement Act (FIRREA). At the end of the third quarter of 1992, the System had 237 more members than when FIRREA was enacted. The system added 657 members through the third quarter 1992, to bring its membership to 3,457. FIRREA allowed banks, credit unions, and other financial institutions meeting QTL tests to become voluntary members of the System.

The post FIRREA period continues to bring additional legislation. In 1991 the Federal Deposit Insurance Corporation Improvement Act was passed. This legislation imposed additional regulations on financial institutions. This act, and other proposed legislation, are viewed as the "backlash" from the debacle. Recent articles and studies point to an impending "banking crisis". The literature on the savings and loan crisis will continue to grow as various related issues have not been settled. The National Commission on Financial Institution Reform, Recovery, and Enforcement is to present its report to Congress in 1993. The purpose of the study is to make recommendations to prevent future problems. Several new books on the topic are slated for publication/release in 1993. The titles of which I am aware are: **Can S&Ls Survive: The Emerging Recovery, Restructuring and Repositioning of America's S&Ls**, by Anat Bird, published by Probus; **The Collapse of Federally Insured Depositories: The Savings and Loan as Precursor**, by R. Dan Brumbaugh, published by Garland Publishing; and **S&L Hell: The People and the Politics Behind the $1 Trillion Savings & Loan Scandal** by Kathleen Day, published by W.W. Norton & Co..

OTHER SOURCES OF INFORMATION

Citations to articles on the crisis are available through numerous online database services. Hard copy indexes such as **Readers' Guide to Periodical Literature, Banking Literature Index,** and **Business Periodicals Index** also provide citations. Due to the massive volume of material printed on the topic it may be advisable to limit initial research to authors who have achieved prominence on this topic. Some of the most quoted articles are: the series written for the **Washington Post** in June 1989 by Rick Atkinson and David Maraniss; Kathleen Day's articles in the **Washington Post;** Pete Brewton's 1988 and 1989 articles in the **Houston Post;** Allen Pusey's 1988 **Dallas Morning News** articles; David LaGesse, Richard Ringer, and others in **American Banker;** Byron Harris' coverage on WFAA Television in Dallas, and articles in the **Wall Street Journal;** **Regardie's Magazine** coverage in December 1987 by William M. Adler and Michael Binstein; **Fortune** November 5, 1990 article by Alan Farnham; the Spring 1990 **Stanford Law and Policy Review 2,** which is an S&L symposium. Specific information on rules and regulations affecting S&Ls can be found in the **Federal Register,** and the **Code of Federal Regulations.** The **Annotated Manual, Examination Manual,** and regulatory bulletins published by the Federal Home Loan Bank Board also contain this information. These items were replaced by the **Regulatory Handbook Series,** containing thrift bulletins and other operating information. The **Series** is now maintained by the Office of Thrift Supervision. The United States League of Savings Institutions published a **Special Management Bulletin** as needed, to discuss rules and regulations. These are detailed summaries and explanations which cover areas such as DIDMCA, Garn-St Germain, direct investments, capital requirements, accounting standards, and classification of assets. Over 300 **Bulletins** have been published which are an excellent source of information on the evolution of thrift regulations. The League also published rules and regulations in a four volume set, the **Federal Guide.** The new name of this association is the Savings & Community Bankers of America, located in Washington, D.C.. Both publications have been continued, retaining the same names.

It is my sincere wish that this volume will aid those conducting research on this topic by helping to identify the documents which will be of the greatest benefit to their endeavors.

ACRONYMS
AND
ABBREVIATIONS

ADC	Acquisition, Development, and Construction
AML	Adjustable Mortgage Loan
ARM	Adjustable Rate Mortgage
BHC	Bank Holding Company
BIF	Bank Insurance Fund
CD	Certificate of Deposit
CEBA	Competitive Equality Banking Act
CRA	Community Reinvestment Act
DIDC	Depository Institutions Deregulation Committee
DIDMCA	Depository Institutions Deregulation and Monetary Control Act
FADA	Federal Asset Disposition Association
FDICIA	Federal Deposit Insurance Corporation Improvement Act
FHFB	Federal Housing Finance Board
FHLBB	Federal Home Loan Bank Board
FHLB System	Federal Home Loan Bank System
FHLMC	Federal Home Loan Mortgage Corporation (Freddie Mac)
FINE	Financial Institutions and the Nation's Economy
FIRREA	Financial Institutions Reform, Recovery, and Enforcement Act
FNMA	Federal National Mortgage Association (Fannie Mae)
FRB	Federal Reserve Board
FSLIC	Federal Savings and Loan Insurance Corporation
GAAP	Generally Accepted Accounting Principles
GAO	Government Accounting Office

GNMA	Government National Mortgage Association (Ginnie Mae)
HMDA	Home Mortgage Disclosure Act
Jumbo CD	Certificate of Deposit over $100,000
MCP	Management Consignment Program
MMMF	Money Market Mutual Fund
NOW accounts	Negotiable Order of Withdrawal
OCC	Office of the Comptroller of the Currency
ODGF	Ohio Deposit Guarantee Fund
OMB	Office of Management and Budget
ORPOS	Office of Regulatory Policy, Oversight, & Supervision (FHLBB)
OTS	Office of Thrift Supervision
PAC	Political Action Committee
QTL	Qualified Thrift Lender
RAP	Regulatory Accounting Principles
REFCORP	Resolution Funding Corporation
RTC	Resolution Trust Corporation
S&Ls	Savings and Loan Associations
SAIF	Savings Association Insurance Fund
TFR	Thrift Financial Report

THE SAVINGS
AND LOAN CRISIS

DEPOSITORY INSTITUTIONS DEREGULATION AND MONETARY CONTROL ACT

1. Cargill, Thomas F. and Gillian G. Garcia. **Financial Deregulation and Monetary Control: Historical Perspective and Impact of the 1980 Act.** Stanford, CA: Hoover Institution Press, 1982. 154 p. index.

The authors were visiting scholars at OCC when the first draft of the Act was written in 1980. They draw on that experience to explain why the act was passed and its possible effects. They state that the Act creates a "level playing field" among deposit institutions. The Act also "removes some of the inequities between large corporate and government users of financial services and the small consumer." They begin with the history of financial reform in the U.S., noting that reform has been both "crisis oriented" and concerned with enhancing the "soundness" of the financial system. They discuss the financial structure dating back to the 1930s, the incompatibility between structure and economic activity in the 1960s, and the major problems of the 1970s. Forces leading to an environment conducive to significant reform are described. The main features of the Act that significantly alter the structure of the financial system are examined. Also presented are comments on the Act's impact on depositories and nondepository intermediaries, and the future viability of financial institutions. The authors also reflect on the need for additional deregulation and further improvement in the conduct of monetary policy. Lastly, they assess the accomplishments of the Act fifteen months after passage. Specifically for S&Ls they discuss interest rate ceilings, sources of funds, use of funds, and expanded powers. An extensive bibliography is included.

2. Colton, Kent W. **Financial Reform: A Review of the Past and Prospects for the Future.** Invited Research Working Paper No. 37. Washington, D.C.: Federal Home Loan Bank Board, September 1980. 44 p.

The author states that the primary factor behind the Depository Institution Deregulation and Monetary Control Act of 1980 was to "legitimate innovations that were already underway at the state and local level." The author reviews the past decade, earlier legislative failures, and the current evolution. Also discussed are possibilities for the future.

3. **Federal Deposit Insurance and the Savings Institution Business.** Washington, D.C.: U.S. League of Savings Institutions, November 1988. 12 p. [3] p.

The Garn-St Germain Act is frequently cited as the beginning of the FSLIC's problems. But it was the Depository Institutions Deregulation and Monetary Control Act of 1980, and "the fact that it preceded asset-side deregulation that is the root of the FSLIC's problems." Savings institutions warned that "hasty removal of rate ceilings carried the potential for financial disaster. Nonetheless, the DIDC ignored . . . warnings and plunged headlong into the deregulation process." Thrifts were forced to dip into reserves to meet interest rate demands and "lost $12B in capital virtually overnight." This paper continues to evaluate the effects of asset-side deregulation on savings institutions. It also seeks to counter the "myth" that S&Ls have moved away from their housing role. A second section of the paper addresses features of the savings institution business which should be preserved including maintaining the FHLB System, distinctive tax provisions, separate regulatory framework, service corporation powers, and equalizing deposit insurance premiums among all depositories. The task force recommended reform through heavy emphasis on capital discipline. The last section of the paper examines "Bailing Out the FSLIC". It calls for an end to the special FSLIC assessment and states that the FHLB System "cannot be considered a source of additional funding." The study states that it will identify alternative sources of additional funds in a forthcoming report.

4. Kane, Edward J. "Reregulation, Savings and Loan Diversification, and the Flow of Housing Finance." In **Savings and Loan Asset Management Under Deregulation**, pp. 81-109. San Francisco: Federal Home Loan Bank of San Francisco, [1981]. 377 p. Proceedings of the Sixth Annual Conference held December 8-9, 1980.

The author begins by stating that the DIDMCA will have a mild effect on profitability and mortgage market participation because, "FSLIC insurance, not deposit rate ceilings, has kept the industry afloat". He points out that the value of FSLIC insurance increases to an institution as its net worth value decreases. Housing finance and industry structure are discussed. The author asserts that the DIDMCA should enhance S&L profitability. The bill opens new opportunities to S&Ls by lifting the state usury limits, and allowing alternative investments. Mr. Kane advocates a freer acquisition policy. This paper was also published as working paper no. 640 by the National Bureau of Economic Research, Inc., March 1981.

5. **Leveling the Playing Field: A Review of the DIDMCA of 1980 and the Garn-St Germain Act of 1982.** Chicago: Federal Reserve Bank of Chicago, December 1983. 54 p.

The DIDMCA and the Garn-St Germain Act contributed to establishing "a more level and competitive playing field." In the mid-80s this terminology was widely used in discussions of the industry. A summary of the Depository Institutions Deregulation and Monetary Control Act of 1980 and the Garn-St Germain Depository Institutions Act of 1982 are presented in this booklet. The DIDMCA was referred to as the most significant banking legislation enacted since the 1930s. Many of the reforms had been suggested in studies conducted from 1961-1975. Inflation and high interest rates finally precipitated legislative action. The principal goals of the DIDMCA are: improving monetary control, and depository institutions sharing in its cost equally; allowing competition for funds and paying small savers a market rate of return; and expanding financial services and reducing competitive inequalities. A history of events leading to the Garn-St Germain Act are given, followed by a discussion of the main features of the act. The act contains eight titles dealing with widening the sources of institution's funds, removal of interest-rate ceilings, expansion of use of funds and powers, and emergency powers for regulators. Included in this review is a discussion of the act's impact on S&Ls, banks, and bank holding companies. This booklet provides an excellent review of the legislation. References are included.

6. McLean, Kenneth A. "Legislative Background of the Depository Institutions Deregulation and Monetary Control Act of 1980." In **Savings and Loan Asset Management Under Deregulation**, pp. 17-30. San Francisco: Federal Home Loan Bank of San Francisco, [1981]. 377 p. Proceedings of the Sixth Annual Conference held December 8-9, 1980.

During passage of the DIDMCA, Mr. McLean was staff director of the U.S. Senate Committee on Banking, Housing, and Urban Affairs. A history of financial restructuring is given with a discussion on why restructuring legislation succeeded after years of failure. Past failures are attributed to the belief that mortgage credit would be affected, and to the various financial trade association rivalries. A discussion of what the bill does and what Congress intended is presented. Not only did the bill include the phase out of deposit rate ceilings, but measures to bolster earnings of thrifts was included. Also the Bank Board was authorized to lower the insurance reserve from 5% to 3%. Deposit insurance was increased, state mortgage usury laws were preempted, and regulators were given the authority to make decisions related to variable-rate mortgages.

7. **1980 Financial Institutions Deregulation and Monetary Control: Public Law 96-221**. Chicago: Commerce Clearing House, Inc., 1989. 253 p. index.

The text begins with a table of effective dates, and table of statutes amended, added or repealed. An explanation with highlights of the Act is presented. Brief explanations of sections of law are given including: powers of thrift institutions, state usury laws, truth in lending, and amendments to national banking laws. The text of the law is included. Selected portions of Congressional committee reports are reproduced in the book. They are presented by topic, with explanations by committee for each topic. Some of the Committee reports referenced are: the Report of the Senate-House Conference Committee HR 96-842; Report of the Senate Committee on Banking, Housing and Urban Affairs on HR 4986 (Senate Report No. 96-368); and Report of the House Committee on Banking, Finance, and Urban Affairs on HR 7 (HR No. 96-263). Topics in this section include: reserves, Regulation Q authority, asset powers, state usury laws, and truth-in-lending.

8. Petersen, Neal L. "The Depository Institutions Deregulation Act (Title II of P.L. 96-221) and Actions of the Depository Institutions Deregulation Committee in Implementing the Act." In **Bank Expansions in the 1980s**, pp. 650-665. New York: Law & Business, Inc., 1982. 777 p. Third Annual Workshop.

Presented in outline format, the findings of Congress and primary and secondary purposes of the Act are given, with references to section numbers included. The various committee meetings are listed; date and committee actions are included.

9. **The Report of the Interagency Task Force on Thrift Institutions**. Committee Print 96-14. Washington, D.C.: U.S. Government Printing Office, 1980. 267 p. Committee on Banking, Finance and Urban Affairs, House of Representatives, 96th Congress, Second Session.

The DIDMCA required the President to appoint a task force to study the problems facing thrift institutions. The task force was to study and make recommendations relating to: thrift asset liability management problems; available options to increase rates paid in inflationary times; and the options available to assist thrifts. The Task Force found that 1980 would be the worst earnings year for thrifts on record, but "in terms of capital and liquidity the thrift industry remains sound . . . ." The Task Force reviewed "what could be done through legislation and/or regulation to assure the long-run position of thrifts in the financial sector." Issues reviewed were interest rate risk, tax structure, federal agencies ability to lend to thrifts, and federal purchase of mortgages.

10. Riordan, Dale P. and Jerry Hartzog. "The Impact of the Deregulation Act on Policy Choices of the Federal Home Loan Bank Board." In **Savings and Loan Asset Management Under Deregulation**, pp. 33-58. San Francisco: Federal Home Loan Bank of San Francisco, [1981]. 377 p. Proceedings of the Sixth Annual Conference held December 8-9, 1980.

The changing industry market will force operational alterations by all depository institutions. The Bank Board will need to adjust by amending policy so associations may respond to market events. The authors assert that the industry's continuity may be in danger without these changes. Restructuring operations and maturity imbalance risk are explored in light of market changes. FHLBB policy issues discussed are asset powers, branching, liabilities, net worth, merger policy, and hedging. The authors advocate a "market-oriented regulatory philosophy" for the FHLBB, and present recommendations for change.

GARN-ST GERMAIN
DEPOSITORY
INSTITUTIONS ACT

11. Cooper, Kerry and Donald R. Fraser. **Banking Deregulation and the New Competition in Financial Service.** Cambridge, MA: Ballinger Publishing Company, 1984. 275 p. index.

A review and analysis of the many changes in the financial industry are presented in this book. In addition to evaluating the new competitive forces, the book offers insights into the future of the industry. The thrift industry is adequately covered in the discussion. Among the related items covered are: activity limitations, loans, demand deposits, interest rates, investments, mergers, failures, and restructuring. Two chapters deal specifically with legislation. In covering the Depository Institutions Deregulation and Monetary Control Act of 1980, it is pointed out that, "This bill represented the first major legislative restructuring of the financial system since the passage of the Banking Act (Glass-Steagall) of 1933." The DIDMCA is "also variously known as the Monetary Control Act of 1980 and the Omnibus Banking Act." A chart shows alternate proposals for change at the congressional level, and includes recommendations which were included in each proposal. The Hunt Commission (President's Commission on Financial Structure and Regulation, 1971) and the FINE report (Financial Institutions and the Nation's Economy, 1975) are discussed as setting the stage for reform. The major provisions of the DIDMCA are discussed in detail. The Garn-St Germain Depository Institutions Act of 1982 also warrants a chapter. The authors point out that although "Garn St Germain has been called the most significant piece of banking legislation to pass Congress in fifty years", it was in fact very narrow in scope. In the short run "Garn St Germain sought to prop up the industry until fundamental changes incorporated . . . could make the industry viable. The long-run component sought to transform radically the nature of the industry." The major provisions of the Act are summarized with particular attention devoted to the effect on the function of the institutions. The remaining chapters deal with deposit insurance and the outlook for deregulation. A bibliography is included.

12. **The Depository Institutions Act of 1982.** Corporate Law and Practice Course Handbook Series No. 406. [New York]: Practising Law Institute, 1983. 400 p.

Raymond Gustini discusses the major provisions of Garn-St Germain, including restructuring, net worth certificates, and new accounts. Other topics covered in this manual are acquisitions and conversions, lending limits, loans to insiders, and preemption of due-on-sale. Thomas P. Vartanian makes lengthy comments in his, "Remarks Regarding the Depository Institutions Act of 1982". He begins with a history of regulation from the nineteenth century, leading to the trend by all regulators to deregulate by 1980. He states that the "Bank Board decided to remove itself from managerial, decision-making processes to the extent legally permissible." He reviews the various facets of deregulation by the Bank Board with brief comments. Footnotes refer to resolution numbers relating to these changes. He also comments on each title of Garn-St Germain and its significance, and then presents a brief synopsis of sections of the Act. Mr. Vartanian states, "With the drop in interest rates and the recent enactment of Garn-St Germain . . . this industry will have the regulatory tools to once again go with the flow of the trend in financial delivery systems and attain profitability."

13. **The Garn-St Germain Depository Institutions Act of 1982: Summary, Text, and Legislative History.** [Washington, D.C.: Federal Home Loan Bank Board, 1982.] [358] p.

Following the summary, this book is divided into several parts. The first part provides a brief description of the legislative history. Questions and answers concerning the Act compose the second part. The full text follows. Parts four through seven contain committee reports on the Act. The reports are: Senate Banking Committee Report on S. 2879; House Banking Committee Report on H.R. 4603 and H.R. 6267; House and Senate consideration and passage of the Conference Report on H.R. 6267; Senate consideration and passage of S. 2879; House consideration and passage of H.R. 4603 and H.R. 6267; and the Senate Banking Committee Report on S. 2607.

14. **New Directions for the Thrift Industry.** Commercial Law and Practice Course Handbook Series No. 310. [New York]: Practising Law Institute, 1983. 880 p.

A synopsis of information in each title of The Garn-St Germain Depository Institutions Act in presented in this handbook. The paper, "Thrifts: New Products and Services" by Bill McBride, presents in outline form information related to increased powers granted by Garn- St Germain. Powers commented on are commercial demand accounts, commercial loans, finance leasing, capital stock and debt, real estate loans, ARMs, and home loans. Mr. McBride also discusses money market deposit accounts, and super-now accounts. "Continued Assistance for the Sick Institutions" is presented by Arthur W. Leibold, Jr. His short outline covers the history of FSLIC financial assistance, and includes primary federal statutory provisions. He also covers eight points related to increases in regulatory net worth and the restructuring of the S&L industry. Daniel P. Kearney discusses accounting innovations and alternative mortgage instruments in his paper, "The Thrift Industry". A copy of H.R. 3537 Financial Institutions Deregulation Act is reproduced in this text.

15. Pafenberg, Forrest W., Frederick E. Flick, and Cynthia A. Hill. **Risk and Regulated Depository Institutions**. Research Paper No. 87-2. Washington, D.C.: National Association of Realtors, November 1987. 77 p.

Thrifts and banks are both covered in this review of depository institutions which focuses on risk. The DIDMCA and Garn-St Germain are discussed. Tables present the changes in S&L asset and liability powers as a result of the legislation. The types of risk inherent in new financial powers are discussed: fraud risk, interest rate risk, securities speculation, managerial, credit, and liquidity risks. The benefits of a thrift charter are reviewed. A chapter is devoted to thrift institution's risk of failure, which encompasses direct investment, asset growth, asset allocation, and nonthrift powers. Similar information is included for commercial banks. Financial information for thrifts and banks is included in the appendix. References are given.

DEPOSIT RATE
CEILINGS

16. Brewer, Elijah, III. **The Impact of Deregulation on the True Cost of Savings Deposits: Evidence from Illinois and Wisconsin Savings and Loan Associations.** Staff Memoranda 85-4. Chicago: Federal Reserve Bank of Chicago, August 1985. 40 p.

Removal of deposit rate ceilings for S&Ls has led to speculation regarding the effect on S&L profitability. This paper focuses on the extent to which ceilings have held down deposit costs. Discussed in detail is the implicit interest paid by S&Ls to attract savings deposits. Forms of implicit interest are deposit taking, money orders, statement maintenance, services below marginal costs, advertising, and gifts for new accounts. Also included are forms of increased customer convenience such as branch offices, ATMs, and lengthening operating hours. Competing for funds through non-rate means increases operating expenses. For the years 1976-1983 the implicit interest rate for institutions increased. This study shows that for Illinois and Wisconsin institutions higher deposit rates could have been paid without adverse effects on profits, because of the resulting lower operating costs. Tables and references are provided in the study.

17. Dann, Larry Y. and Christopher M. James. **An Analysis of the Impact of Deposit Rate Ceilings on the Market Values of Stock Savings and Loan Associations.** Staff Papers 1981-4. Washington, D.C. : Comptroller of the Currency, 1981. 30 p.

The impact of deposit rate regulations on the value of S&Ls is examined. Regulation of interest rates on deposits in S&Ls began in 1966. In 1980, the DIDMCA was passed to phase out the ceilings. The analysis reflects that S&L's

common stockholders have earned negative returns after the announcement of ceiling rate removals. The authors assert that this supports the hypothesis that "S&Ls have earned economic rents from the restrictions on interest rates paid to small saver accounts and that relaxation of interest rate ceilings has reduced those rents." Three distinct instances of regulatory change were examined and the evidence shows that "interest rate ceilings have been administered by federal regulatory agencies in such a way as to reduce the subsidy to thrift institutions." References are included.

18. Gray, Jonathan E. **Financial Deregulation and the Savings and Loan Crisis.** New York: Sanford Bernstein & Co., Inc., December 1988. 38 p.

This report was prepared at the request of the FDIC. The author traces the connections between deregulation and the S&L problems. He states that, "deposit decontrol was perhaps the single most important cause" of the steep interest rate rise and the bad loan problem. He also discusses the effects of deregulation on the consumer and the ability of the Federal Reserve to control the economy.

19. Hess, Alan C. **Effects of Regulation Q On Deposits and Interest Rates at Savings Associations.** RWP 83-04. Kansas City, MO: Federal Reserve Bank of Kansas City, March 1983. 24 p.

Interest rate ceilings were imposed to preserve S&L's competitiveness, thus ensuring a flow of mortgage money. Mr. Hess states that "the legislation was based on wrong assumptions" and that "neither the deposit flows nor rates paid were affected by Regulation Q." References are given.

20. Hess, Alan C. and Daniel J. Vrabac. **Regulation Q and the Profitability of Savings Associations.** RWP 83-03. Kansas City, MO: Federal Reserve Bank of Kansas City, March 1983. 18 p.

The effects of Regulation Q on the profitability of savings associations from 1950-1979 are presented in this paper. Regulation Q interest rate ceilings were to be slowly removed based on the effect on S&Ls. Hess and Vrabac examine the arguments against removal presented by the S&L industry. The authors state that Regulation Q has no effect on profitability and delay in its removal is unnecessary. References are included.

21. Marcis, Richard G. "Implications of Financial Innovation and Reform for the Savings and Loan Industry." In **The Savings and Loan Industry in the 1980s**, pp. [11-24]. Research Working Paper No. 100. Washington, D.C.: Federal Home Loan Bank Board, December 1980. [43] p.

Mr. Marcis was the chief economist of the FHLBB. His paper relates to increased competition in the 1980s and the removal of deposit rate controls. He also comments on the "problem area" of capital adequacy in the industry.

MORTGAGE LENDING

22. Carron, Andrew S. and R. Dan Brumbaugh, Jr. **The Future of Thrifts in the Mortgage Market.** [n.p.]: The First Boston Corporation, December 1988. 17 p. Presentation at the Annual Meeting of the American Economic Association, New York.

Thrifts have traditionally originated about half of all residential mortgage loans in the U.S. Laws and regulations required them to invest in mortgage loans, and other incentives encouraged this investment. Certain other investments were prohibited. This paper reviews thrift performance and requirements for mortgage market participation. The authors state, "We conclude that thrifts can earn a reasonable rate of return on virtually all activities except the one they are required to undertake: portfolio lending. Policies toward thrifts intended to promote housing may even have the opposite effect." Charts and graphs are included in the paper's exploration of thrift viability related to mortgage loans. The authors conclude, "The only viable solution for the future is removing the requirement that thrifts hold 60 percent of their total assets in housing related instruments. The qualified thrift lender test should be eliminated, or at least rationalized to give full weight to originations rather than holdings of mortgages." This paper was also presented at the 25th Annual Conference on Bank Structure and Competition sponsored by the Federal Reserve Bank of Chicago, May 3-5, 1989. It is published in the conference proceedings, **Banking System Risk: Charting a New Course,** pp. 385-400.

23. Cassidy, Henry J. "The Effects of Due-on-Sale on Mortgage Interest Rates." Technical Paper No. 3. In **Final Report and Technical Papers of the Task Force On Due-On-Sale,** pp. [69-111]. Washington, D.C.: Federal Home Loan Bank Board, March 1982. 121 p.

Mr. Cassidy states that eliminating the due-on-sale clause will lead to higher mortgage rates. An options pricing model and a computer simulation model were both used for analysis. Assumability differentials in the range of 30-90 basis points were found. The "most likely" assumption produced an assumability differential of 50 basis points.

24. Chamberlain, Charlotte, A. Thomas King, Mark Meador and Larry Ozanne. "Structure of the Savings and Loan Industry." Technical Paper No. 1. In **Final Report and Technical Papers of the Task Force On Due-On-Sale**, pp. [28-39]. Washington, D.C.: Federal Home Loan Bank Board, March 1982. 121 p.

A financial profile of the S&L industry is presented. Assets and liabilities as they relate to the mortgage portfolio are reviewed; several tables provide statistics back to the early 1970s. Additional tables reflect the financial loss to S&Ls from mortgages made at low interest rates as market rates increase, and losses due to prohibition of due-on-sale.

25. Federal Savings and Loan Advisory Council. **How Can Savings and Loans be Profitable While Concentrating on Housing Finance?** Cincinnati: Federal Home Loan Bank of Cincinnati, December 1984. 106 p.

The Council studied the impediments to S&L profitability in housing; and presented solutions and opportunities for growth. The study contains discussion on managing interest rate risk. Also offered are policy recommendations. Tables related to S&L mortgage lending, supply, and projected demand are included. References are provided.

26. **Final Report and Technical Papers of the Task Force On Due-On-Sale**. Washington, D.C.: Federal Home Loan Bank Board, March 1982. 121 p.

A twenty-seven page summary of the task force findings is given. The summary states that "Prohibition of due-on-sale provides no net social benefit." It also states that removal of the prohibition is necessary to reduce expected S&L losses. The report discusses how future mortgage borrowers are adversely affected by the prohibition. The report also includes four technical papers which explore the topic in detail.

27. Fraser, Donald R. **The Changing Role of Depository Financial Institutions and the Availability of Funds to the Real Estate Industry**. Technical Report. College Station, TX: Texas A&M University, August 1981. 80 p.

The decline in total credit provided by depository institutions, and decline in share of flow of funds is discussed in this paper. Competition from non-depository institutions is reviewed. The blurring of lines between depository institutions is affecting the real estate market. The author points out that society has changed since the creation of the depository institution structure; the institutions should be expected to change as well. Charts show the change in portfolio composition at S&Ls, banks, and credit unions from 1946-1980. For S&Ls the greatest change is the reduction of the passbook account, and the increase in the use of certificate accounts. Tables reflect the ownership of mortgages from 1946-1980. The Depository Institutions Deregulations and Monetary Control Act of 1980 is discussed in some detail. Presented are the specifics of the act, its background and reason for passage, and its implications. Mr. Fraser comments that several recommendations were not included in the DIDMCA, including branching, regulatory framework, equality of regulation, and availability of mortgage credit. He notes, "The failure to address these issues makes it likely that there will be further legislation affecting the structure of financial institutions." The author examines the concerns that S&Ls will be "unable or unwilling" to provide mortgage funds as the industry changes. He discusses several studies and presents charts compiled by the FHLBB which project the liability structure of S&Ls under various interest rate scenarios for the years 1980-1988. The paper concludes, "Econometric simulations of previous proposals for financial reform suggest no long-term negative impact on the mortgage market of financial reform."

28. Hendershott, Patric H. "The Future of Thrifts as Home Mortgage Portfolio Lenders." In **The Future of the Thrift industry**, pp. 153-163. San Francisco: Federal Home Loan Bank of San Francisco, 1989. 253 p. Proceedings of the Fourteenth Annual Conference, December 8-9, 1988.

The fundamental problem threatening thrifts, as portfolio lenders in the future, is that mortgage yields are inadequate for the cost structure of profitable thrifts and will continue to be so. The paper discusses the lowered mortgage yields caused by GNMA, FNMA, and FHLMC, asserting that yields have been lowered in more than half of the residential mortgage markets. Also discussed is the response thrifts should make to the yield squeeze. The author suggests, "Thrifts must reduce their cost structure and persuade Congress either to raise the agency cost structure or limit the agencies' presence in the mortgage market."

29. Hirschhorn, Eric. **Profiles in Profitability**. Washington, D.C.: Office of Thrift Supervision, March 1990. [8] p.

Profitable thrifts are compared with less profitable thrifts for the period of 1985 through third quarter 1989. The author notes that FIRREA will drive all thrifts to resemble the profitable thrifts, and their experience demonstrates how institutions can compete successfully. He states that the most profitable group of thrifts has been stable from one year to another. Their balance sheet structure reflects "a greater commitment to traditional portfolio lending and a heavier reliance on traditional funding sources." On the asset side the profitable thrifts held more 1-4 family mortgages. Charts illustrate the text. Mr. Hirschhorn concludes by stating, "the traditional activities of the thrift industry can provide an attractive return on equity . . . institutions that conform to the new rules can compete successfully. . . ."

30. **How Can Savings and Loans Be Profitable While Concentrating on Housing Finance?** [Washington, D.C.]: Federal Savings and Loan Advisory Council, Specialized Housing Lender Subcommittee, December 1984. 101 p. [5] p.

The focus of this report is on the problems S&Ls face in continuing as a dominant force in housing finance. The solutions to the problems are discussed. The report concludes that it is possible to be aggressive and profitable in the market. The committee makes specific recommendations, i.e. restoring capital/risk discipline, expansion of new business powers, and access to electronic mortgage origination networks. Tables, charts, and references are part of the text.

31. Jaffee, Dwight M. "The Future Role of Thrift Institutions in Mortgage Lending." In **The Future of the Thrift Industry**, pp. 164-180. Conference Series No. 24. Boston: Federal Reserve Bank of Boston, [1982]. 187 p. Proceedings of a Conference held October 1981.

Alternative mortgage-lending strategies are discussed from the perspective of the impact they could have on an institution's continued viability. The costs and benefits are analyzed. Affecting the strategies are deposit flows, changes in the market, and the economy. The two lending strategies discussed are portfolio lending and mortgage banking. The author concludes by stating, "hedging interest rate risks, and innovating secondary market trading, will be the hallmarks of successful S&L lending in the 1980s."

32. Meador, Mark. **The Effects on Mortgage Repayments of Restrictions on the Enforcement of Due-on-Sale Clauses: Aggregate and Micro California Results**. Research Working Paper No. 107. Washington, D.C.: Federal Home Loan Bank Board, August 1982. 19 p.

Enforcement restrictions add to the financial distress of thrifts. Eighteen states have restrictions on the enforcement of due-on-sale clauses. This paper examines the California S&Ls repayment experience with due-on-sale restrictions. The author states that the "estimates imply large income losses for California state-chartered" S&Ls. His figures show that repayments would have provided a substantial income flow per year. Mr. Meador concludes, "the restrictions on the enforcement of due-on-sale clauses have hampered the ability of state associations to adjust their mortgage portfolio yields and have added to the losses imposed by the recent unexpected rise in interest rates."

33. Meador, Mark, Larry Ozanne, and Donald Edwards. "Estimating the Impact of Due-on-Sale Restrictions on S&L Earnings." Technical Paper No. 2. In **Final Report and Technical Papers of the Task Force On Due-On-Sale**, pp. [40-68]. Washington, D.C.: Federal Home Loan Bank Board, March 1982. 121 p.

This paper served as the basis for the S&L earnings impact discussed in the Task Force report. The estimates were based partly on a survey, which was combined with mortgage repayment analysis, and applied through simulators. The survey revealed an increase of due-on-sale clauses included in mortgages from 71% in 1967 to 83% in 1981. The survey also reflects enforcement trends. The study shows that repayment rates in California declined as interest rates rose. A sixteen page appendix to this paper written by Mark Meador is entitled, "Repayment Rate Effects of Due-on-Sale Restrictions." The effect of the California Wallenkamp decision on state-chartered S&Ls is detailed.

34. Ozanne, Larry. **The Financial Stakes in Due-on-Sale: The Case of California's State-Chartered Savings and Loans**. Research Working Paper No. 109. Washington, D.C.: Federal Home Loan Bank Board, July 1982. 31 p.

The importance of the clause is illustrated by Mr. Ozanne's calculations. He estimates that in 1981, $58-$170 million was lost by S&Ls unable to enforce the clause in California. This was between a tenth and a quarter of the total 1981 S&L losses in that state. A 1978 California Supreme Court ruling enforced loans from state chartered lenders as assumable. In 1982 the U.S. Supreme Court ruled that federally chartered S&Ls were protected from this ruling because due-on-sale was important to the financial soundness of lenders. References are included.

35. Shontell, Jayne, Stephen Schoepke, and Henry J. Cassidy. "Effects of State Due-on-Sale Restrictions on the Secondary Mortgage Market." Technical Paper No. 4. In **Final Report and Technical Papers of the Task Force On**

Due-On-Sale, pp. [112-121]. Washington, D.C.: Federal Home Loan Bank Board, March 1982. 121 p.

Mr. Shontell and Mr. Schoepke were with the Federal Home Loan Mortgage Corporation when the paper was written. The authors state that investors assume a greater proportion of the risk for mortgages without enforceable clauses, which may lead to lower investment returns. This risk leads to discounts on mortgage-backed securities, and a reallocation of funds away from the housing industry to more stable investments.

36. Vartanian, Thomas P. "Developments in the Savings and Loan Industry." In **Legal Problems of Bank Regulation 1981**, pp. 29-40. New York: Law Journal Seminars-Press, 1981. 800 p. Eighth Annual Conference.

Mr. Vartanian explains that the Bank Board has "undertaken a 'zero-based' review of the regulatory framework" of insured institutions "for the purposes of continuing the deregulation of the savings and loan industry initiated under the Depository Institutions Deregulation and Monetary Control Act of 1980." The emphasis of this paper is on adjustable mortgage loans and other new mortgage instruments including graduated payment AMLs, balloon payment loans, flexible payment loans, and the pledged account loan. In outline form the major elements of each type of proposed AML is presented. Also discussed are interstate activities, service corporation investments, and futures transactions.

37. Weicher, John C. "The Future Structure of the Housing Finance System." In **Restructuring Banking & Financial Services in America**, pp. 296-336. Edited by William S. Haraf and Rose Marie Kushmeider. Washington, D.C.: American Enterprise Institute for Public Policy Research, 1988. 494 p. index.

The history of S&Ls and their role in housing is reviewed. The financial situation of S&Ls as affected by inflation and interest rates is discussed. FSLIC recapitalization and its possible effect on thrifts is reviewed. The author points out that diversification has shifted thrifts away from mortgage lending, stating that, "From 1979 to 1986, mortgages and mortgage securities declined from 86 to 68 percent of S&L assets . . . ." Several pages of this paper are devoted to a discussion of the secondary market agencies. The author concludes by considering the question, "Is housing special?" He states, "There is surely still a substantial social preference for housing. That preference . . . perhaps cannot any longer be achieved by channeling credit to housing."

ACCOUNTING AND TAX ISSUES

38. Benston, George J., Mike Carhill, and Brian Olasov. "Market Value versus Historical Cost Accounting: Evidence from Southeastern Thrifts." In **The Reform of Federal Deposit Insurance: Disciplining the Government and Protecting Taxpayers**, pp. 277-304. Edited by James R. Barth and R. Dan Brumbaugh. [N.Y.]: HarperBusiness, 1992. 310 p. index.

Year end market values are estimated from aggregated financial information filed with the FHLBB and OTS for 517 thrifts which were members of the FHLB-Atlanta on 12-31-84. In 1984 "Section H" was added to the thrift financial reports. In this section contracted nominal annual rates and maturities of assets and liabilities are reported. Using this information the authors are able to estimate market values for the financial assets and liabilities held by thrifts. An overview of the methodology is presented. Tables reflect related financial figures. The authors state, "The results reported here show that market valuation applied generically is superior to traditional accounting methodologies applied on thrifts specifically."

39. **Current Tax Rules Relating to Financially Troubled Savings and Loan Associations: Scheduled for Hearings Before the House Committee on Ways and Means on February 22 and March 9, 1989**. Washington, D.C.: Joint Committee on Taxation, February 16, 1989. 50 p.

The first part of the pamphlet discusses the industry, FSLIC, and the potential budget implications of the thrift problems. The current tax laws which apply to thrifts are presented. The last part of the pamphlet discusses issues related to using the tax system to provide benefits to deposit insurers.

40. **Economic Implications of a Tax Credit Program to Facilitate the Sale of RTC Property.** Washington, D.C.: GRC Economics, September 1990. 17 p.

Asserted in this paper are the benefits of a tax credit program to expedite the sale of property by the RTC. The benefits listed are to save taxpayers money, stimulate the economy, and to create jobs. Holding costs escalate the longer property is held by the government, and a "fire sale" is damaging to real estate values. For every $1 of tax credit, $2 in revenue is generated. The paper states, "At the end of April 1990 the RTC held title to 37,082 properties with a book value of $13.9 billion." They speculate that the value of the properties will decline the longer they are held by the RTC. GRC Economics, the consulting unit of Hill and Knowlton, Inc., evaluates the economic costs and benefits of a tax credit program. The details of the program are described in the paper.

41. Finegan, Patrick G. **Master Financial Statements: Who Murdered Savings & Loans.** Washington, D.C.: Palindrome Press, 1991. 203 p. index.

A mixture of philosophy and educational insights to financial statements is presented. The author explores financial statements, the role of auditors and accounting firms, and how numbers can be manipulated. References to S&Ls are interspersed with many personal opinions.

42. Goodman, Rae Jean B. **An Assessment of Recent Changes and Proposals in S&L Taxation.** Invited Research Working Paper No. 43. Washington, D.C.: Federal Home Loan Bank Board, September 1983. 28 p.

An analysis of the effects of several events is presented in this paper. The Tax Equity and Fiscal Responsibility Act of 1982, the Garn-St Germain Depository Institutions Act of 1982, and the President's Commission on Housing's proposed mortgage interest tax credit are examined. The results show that the Tax Equity Act will increase S&L tax liability by 10-40%. Garn-St Germain will increase taxes slightly if S&Ls act as savings banks, and the mortgage interest tax credit will increase liability by 35-81%. Tables are included.

43. Goodman, Rae Jean B. **Savings and Loan Association Taxation: History, Issues and Alternatives.** Invited Research Working Paper No. 32. Washington, D.C.: Federal Home Loan Bank Board, February 1980. 86 p.

Tax treatment of S&Ls is reviewed in support of the FHLBB's goal to develop a tax policy which addresses the impact of taxation on the industry and on housing finance. A comparison of tax treatment of S&Ls, mutual savings banks, and commercial banks is presented. A chart shows tax as a percent of economic income for these three groups of institutions. A discussion of the tax issues of S&L conversions and leasing operations is included. The author states that the tax burden borne by S&Ls is high compared to other institutions. Alternative policy options are explored. Various mortgage tax credits and incentives are discussed with charts presenting supporting data. It is noted that the treasury "would have to take a substantial revenue loss to affect savings flows." The appendices include treasury proposals and the implication for the industry, and a description of congressional bills for tax incentives. References are given.

44. **Issue Summary: Accounting for Savings and Loan Associations Under FSLIC Management Consignment Program (MCP).** EITF 85-41. [New York]: Emerging Issues Task Force, 1985. 7 p.

This summary provides questions and answers related to MCP accounting issues. The summary was prepared by the Federal Home Loan Bank Board. A copy of R 55 related to push-down accounting is included in the summary.

45. Kuhn, Gerald J. **A Summarization of RAP and GAAP for FSLIC-Insured Thrift Institutions.** Chicago: Financial Managers Society, Inc., March 1983. 11 p.

This paper reviews accounting areas in which there are conflicts between RAP and GAAP. References to regulations and FHLBB memoranda are included. References to supportive documentation for GAAP are presented.

46. **Report of the Expanded Task Force on Current Value Accounting.** [Washington, D.C.: Federal Home Loan Bank Board], April 12, 1983. [45] p.

FHLBB Chairman Pratt formed an interoffice task force on market value accounting on July 19, 1982. The charge to the group was to develop a proposal for a market value accounting system that would reflect the substance of S&L transactions. A proposed regulation was sent out for comment as a result of the task force on November 4, 1982, but was withdrawn due to industry concerns. The chairman then formed the expanded task force which included representatives outside of FHLBB staff. The task force objectives included considering the consequences of interest rate volatility, and the problems of cost accounting. Their recommendations were based on those objectives. The recommendations included: adopting a system for reporting interest sensitivity; testing the new reporting on a pilot group of institutions; analyzing duration, gap, and spread from institution reporting; testing current value accounting; and applying current value accounting to all financial institutions. Information on the pilot program, and the framework for testing current value accounting is included. A section on valuation of financial assets and liabilities is presented.

47. **Report of the Task Force on Savings and Loan Portfolio Profitability.** Little Rock, AR: Federal Home Loan Bank of Little Rock, July 1981. 87 p.

Often referred to as the "Settle report", for the President of the Bank at the time it was written, this report was prepared for the FHLB-Little Rock and the FHLBB. Recognizing the industry problem of duration imbalance, the task force explored corrective actions. It notes that 265 institutions were listed as "problems" at the end of May 1981. At the end of 1980 industry book value net worth far exceeded its market value. One of the primary standards set by the task force was that "no formal federal bailouts will be considered or proposed in this study." The study focuses on GAAP and RAP and related accounting issues. This study is a detailed examination of industry problems, and presents recommendations for dealing with them.

48.   **Revised Report of the Interoffice Task Force on Market Value Accounting.** Washington, D.C.: Federal Home Loan Bank Board, October 8, 1982. [52] p.

This is a revision of the preliminary report of the task force after receiving comments from the industry and others. The proposal requires adjusting all assets and liabilities with a term to maturity of one year or more to their estimated current value at the end of each quarter. The task force also recommended changes to the accounting provisions of the interest rate futures and options regulations to include unrealized gains or losses in current value computations. The second section of the paper summarizes the comments and changes to the preliminary report. A discussion of the recommendations is included. A table of market discount rates and simulation results are presented.

49. Robbins, Aldona, and Gary Robbins. **How Tax Policy Compounded the S&L Crisis.** Lewisville, TX: Institute for Policy Innovation, 1991. 33 p.

Many institutions with real estate investments were weakened by the 1986 Tax Reform Act. The affect of the Act on the real estate market is described in this paper. The study notes that "tax changes reduced the value of commercial real estate by 17 percent and the value of owner-occupied real estate by 9 percent." The authors speculate that raising the capital gains tax rate and deferring real estate tax deductions may have pushed "beleaguered S&Ls" to greater losses. It is suggested that these tax policies should be reexamined. An appendix presents a standard framework for real estate investment analysis.

50. **Savings and Loan Asset Restructuring and Reinvestment Considerations.** n.p.: Arthur Young & Co., 1982. [65] p. A program sponsored by the FHLB Little Rock, September 28-29, 1982 in Dallas, Texas.

Several documents are included in this booklet. An Arthur Young Client Memorandum, "Accounting for Mergers of Thrift Institutions", reviews accounting aspects. The memorandum comments on acquisitions without cash, governmental inducements, and application of the purchase method. Other Arthur Young documents discuss a possible amendment to APB Opinion No. 17, loss deferrals on the sale of mortgage loans, and mark to market. The August 27, 1982 **Preliminary Report of the Interoffice Task Force on Market Value Accounting**, issued by the FHLBB, is included in the booklet. An official news release from the New Jersey department of banking proposing mark to market accounting is reproduced. Also included is a news release from the Pennsylvania department of banking granting permission to use asset restatement accounting.

DEPOSIT INSURANCE

51. Barth, James R. "Post-FIRREA: The Need to Reform the Federal Deposit Insurance System." In **Game Plans for the '90s**, pp. 333-351. Chicago: Federal Reserve Bank of Chicago, 1990. 638 p. The 26th Annual Conference on Bank Structure and Competition, May 9-11, 1990.

Mr. Barth reviews the causes of the S&L crisis, and the insufficient governmental response to the problems. He states, "It is my view that the major culprit in the savings and loan crisis is federal deposit insurance." The changes mandated by FIRREA are discussed. The author asserts that deposit insurance must be reformed to protect taxpayers. He proposes: assessment of market-based information and timely closings of inadequately capitalized institutions; market discipline; cross-guarantees; reinsurance; and requiring all insured deposits be backed by "riskless assets." References are included.

52. Barth, James R. **Thrift Deregulation and Federal Deposit Insurance.** Research Paper No. 150. Washington, D.C.: Federal Home Loan Bank Board, November 1988. 60 p.

Mr. Barth argues that federal deposit insurance must be covered by a "rule" which would cover catastrophic losses. He also asserts that S&L charters have value and are worth preserving. This paper explores these topics in detail. References are given.

53. Barth, James R. and R. Dan Brumbaugh, Jr., eds. **The Reform of Federal Deposit Insurance: Disciplining the Government and Protecting Taxpayers.** [N.Y.]: HarperBusiness, 1992. 310 p. index.

This volume is the result of a conference on this topic which was sponsored by the Center for Economic Policy Research at Stanford University in 1990. The contributors are economists, well known for their views on deposit insurance and the industry. Both editors are former economists with the Federal Home Loan Bank Board. Counting the introduction, eleven papers are included. Among the authors are George Benston, Edward Kane, and George Kaufman. Tables, charts, and figures are located throughout the text. References are included in the majority of the papers. This book provides a useful review of the industry from a current perspective.

54. Barth, James R., et al. **Alternative Federal Deposit Insurance Regimes.** Research Paper No. 152. Washington, D.C.: Federal Home Loan Bank Board, January 1989. 39 p.

The history of deposit insurance is traced. FSLIC and FDIC coverage is discussed. Information on the reserves and costs incurred for both funds is given. Calculations are provided for the effect additional assessments might have had on FSLIC. Charts, graphs, and tables are included. Especially interesting are tables presenting information on thrift failures from 1934-1987.

55. Barth, James R., Michael G. Bradley, and John J. Feid. **The Federal Deposit Insurance System: Origins and Omissions.** Research Paper No. 153. Washington, D.C.: Federal Home Loan Bank Board, January 1989. 20 p.

The value of the thrift charter has been obscured by the focus on troubled thrifts. In their discussion of FSLIC the authors make the point that it should be reformed. They stress that GAAP-solvent thrift's ROE has exceeded that at banks, making their charters worth retaining.

56. Barth, James R. and Philip F. Bartholomew. "The Thrift Industry Crisis: Revealed Weaknesses in the Federal Deposit Insurance System." In **The Reform of Federal Deposit Insurance: Disciplining the Government and Protecting Taxpayers,** pp. 36-116. Edited by James R. Barth and R. Dan Brumbaugh. [N.Y.]: HarperBusiness, 1992. 310 p. index.

The authors argue that the "major culprit in the thrift crisis is the current structure of the insurance system", and that the greatest shortcoming in FIRREA is its failure to restructure the insurance system. The discussion includes a short history of the crisis, the costs, and government's response. Tables show a history of FIRREA, thrift industry financial data from 1980-1989, and insolvencies by state and institution. An interesting table lists estimates of cost of resolving the thrift crisis. The list shows the source of the estimate, the estimated cost, and a short description. The authors give their suggestions for deposit insurance reform. Extensive references are given. A lengthy appendix lists all tangible insolvent thrift institutions as of 12-31-89. The list provides docket number, name, length of insolvency, tangible net worth, tangible assets, GAAP net worth, and GAAP assets.

57. Benston, George J., et al. **Perspectives on Safe & Sound Banking: Past, Present, and Future.** Series on the regulation of economic activity. Cambridge, MA: MIT Press, 1986. 358 p. index. A study commissioned by the American Bankers Association.

Concern over the growing number of problem banks led the ABA to commission a study on safety and soundness issues. An oversight committee composed of bankers selected five academic consultants to conduct the study. The consultants were George Benston, Robert Eisenbeis, Paul Horvitz, Edward Kane, and George Kaufman. While S&Ls are only mentioned peripherally in this text, the discussions of deposit insurance, regulatory oversight, and market value accounting are valuable sources of information. Extensive references are provided at the end of the text.

58. **Blueprint for Restructuring America's Financial Institutions: Report of a Task Force.** Washington, D.C.: The Brookings Institution, 1989. 31 p.

The task force members have all offered restructuring proposals. The members are George Benston, R. Dan Brumbaugh, Jr., Jack Guttentag, Richard Herring, George Kaufman, Robert Litan, and Kenneth Scott. Each of the proposals shared some common ground which led the authors to develop a joint proposal for restructuring the regulatory and deposit insurance systems. The solutions recommended apply to all depository institutions. The authors identify four flaws in the current system: deposit insurance encourages risk-taking; regulators have been unable to detect excessive risk exposure; authorities have not intervened in weak institutions early enough; and interventions have protected all depositors not just the insured. The structural reform objectives offered are: maintain safety of insured deposits; strengthen market discipline on risk exposure; enhance efficiency by eliminating some restriction on powers, and minimize costs of necessary restrictions; prompt disposition of insolvent institutions; and minimize transition costs by allowing institutions to choose one of two options. The authors urge the acceptance of a new system immediately. A bibliography of each of the author's individual proposals is included.

59. Brewer, Elijah, III. **The Impact of Deposit Insurance on S & L Shareholders' Risk/Return Trade-Offs.** Working Paper 89-24. Chicago: Federal Reserve Bank of Chicago, December 1989. 33 p.

This paper tests the hypothesis that insured institutions shift risk to deposit insurance by investing in assets to increase the value of shareholder equity. The author examines the impact of balance sheet changes on S&L common stock returns. Data for the July 1984-December 1987 period is used. The behavior of high-risk S&Ls was compared to low-risk S&Ls. The author states the results show that deposit insurance provides incentives to shift from low-risk to high-risk investments. References and tables are included.

60. Burnham, James B. **A Financial System for the Year 2000: The Case for Narrow Banking**. Center for the Study of American Business Formal Publication No. 97. St. Louis, MO: Washington University, February 1990. 28 p.

This study focuses on the financial sector covered by deposit insurance. The author proposes limiting deposit insurance to only "narrow banks", those whose investment opportunities are severely limited. He further suggests that only "narrow banks" should have access to the Federal Reserve's payments system. He reviews and comments on other reform proposals.

61. Congressional Budget Office. **Budgetary Treatment of Deposit Insurance: A Framework for Reform**. [Washington, D.C.]: Congressional Budget Office, May 1991. 78 p.

The Omnibus Budget Reconciliation Act of 1990 directed CBO to "study whether the accounting for federal deposit insurance programs should be on a cash basis, on the same basis as loan guarantees, or on a different basis." The study states that FSLIC's budgetary treatment did not give timely warning and thus contributed to the disaster. The government's ability to recognize events as they occur will prevent similar occurrences in the future. The report discusses several options in detail: maintain current policy, create an account for working capital, link accrued deficits to fee adjustments, transform insurance funds into government-sponsored enterprises, or recognize past losses. The CBO does not recommend policy action, but presents options. Many tables and charts are included. One table reflects net outlays for federal deposit insurance from 1977-1996 for banks, thrifts, and credit unions. Among other tables are: total deficit with and without deposit insurance for 1975-1996; effective insurance premiums for deposit insurance funds 1970-1989; and annual budgetary resources for deposit insurance 1986-1992.

62. **Deposit Insurance in a Changing Environment**. Washington, D.C.: Federal Deposit Insurance Corporation, April 15, 1983. [205] p.

A study of deposit insurance was mandated by the Garn-St Germain Depository Institutions Act of 1982. The FDIC study has two major themes. The first is "to impose a greater degree of marketplace discipline on the system to replace outmoded government controls." The second theme is to make the insurance system "as effective, efficient and equitable as possible." The book is divided into seven chapters. The chapters cover these topics: current system of insurance; risk related premiums; market discipline and the insurance system; public disclosure practices; fund adequacy; merger of funds; and optional excess deposit insurance. Bibliographies are provided on risk related insurance systems for banks, and on failure prediction models.

63. Ely, Bert and Vicki Vanderhoff. **Lessons Learned from the S&L Debacle: The Price of Failed Public Policy.** IPI Policy Report No. 108. Lewisville, TX: The Institute for Policy Innovation, February 1991. 36 p.

Bert Ely was one of the early predictors of the FSLIC bankruptcy. This report points to deposit insurance as the root of the S&L debacle. Examined are the federal and state policies which contributed to the failures.

64. Federal Home Loan Bank Board. **Agenda for Reform: A Report on Deposit Insurance to the Congress from the Federal Home Loan Bank Board.** Washington, D.C.: Federal Home Loan Bank Board, March 23, 1983. 416 p.

A major study of deposit insurance was mandated by the Garn-St Germain Depository Institutions Act of 1982. This study was prepared in response to that mandate; its premise is that the system must be reformed or re-regulated. The Bank Board oversaw development of the policy aspects of the study; prominent economists prepared the manuscripts which were reviewed by commentators. The focus of the study was the impact of deposit insurance on depository institutions, the feasibility of risk-based insurance, the adequacy of public disclosure, the impact of expanding coverage, and the feasibility of consolidating insurance funds. The recommendations covered accounting and disclosure, variable-rate premiums, private insurance, fiduciary responsibility, capital adequacy, and regulatory reform. Detailed commentary is provided on the issues involved in the recommendations. This study provides an excellent view of the industry in the early 1980s. The contributors are among those authors who became most prolific on the subject. Bibliographies and references are included.

65. Guttentag, Jack and Richard Herring. "The Insolvency of Financial Institutions: Assessment and Regulatory Disposition." In **Crises in the**

Economic and Financial Structure, pp. 99-126. Edited by Paul Wachtel. Lexington, MA: Lexington Books, 1982. 344 p. index.

Elimination of bank runs through deposit insurance, and regulator's solvency determinations is the theme of this paper. The focus is on S&Ls and how errors in solvency determinations are made using traditional criteria. They note that thrifts may engage in "dysfunctional" behavior if their book net worth is under pressure. The authors discuss appropriate disposition decisions, as well as the need for a new type of capital assistance. References are incorporated.

66. Heller, Warren G. **Is Your Money Safe?: How to Protect Your Savings in the Current Banking Crisis.** New York: Berkley Books, 1990. 112 p.

Written by the Research Director of Veribanc, Inc., a bank ranking service, S&L problems are described. The author states that he uses the term "bank" to encompass all financial institutions. He first describes the "banking" business and how the crisis began. He discusses bank problems with loans to third world countries, the real estate crash, junk bonds, dishonesty, and incompetence. A chapter is devoted to deposit insurance wherein bank closures are described, and a chart reflecting the strength of the three insurance funds is provided, as well as information on state insurance funds. The following three chapters cover: institutions in trouble, warning signals; risks in dealing with banks; and how to choose the safest bank. Lists of the safest banks are included. A list of S&Ls with foreclosed property is given in a chapter dealing with opportunities in banking. The appendix contains a list of agency contacts for complaints.

67. Kane, Edward J. "Confronting Incentive Problems in U.S. Deposit Insurance: The Range of Alternative Solutions." In **Deregulating Financial Services: Public Policy in Flux**, pp. 97-120. Edited by George G. Kaufman and Roger C. Kormendi. Cambridge, MA: Ballinger Publishing Co., 1986. 223 p.

The author argues that GAAP distorts the perception of a financial institution's earnings and understates bailout costs. He calls for a redesign of deposit insurance to decrease risk taking, and presents six proposals for reform. Mr. Kane calls for market-value accounting and risk-related premiums. He also comments on the "political dilemma of reform". References are included at the end of the paper.

68. Kane, Edward J. **The Gathering Crisis in Federal Deposit Insurance.** MIT Press series on the regulation of economic activity No. 11. Cambridge, MA: The MIT Press, 1985. 176 p. index.

Using analogies which should be understood by most, Mr. Kane explains the break down in deposit insurance and why it is of concern. He notes that the financial system of the U.S. cannot be "controlled effectively" without solving the deposit insurance problem. He also comments on the many hearings related to deposit insurance and the lack of action by Congress. "In refusing to act on the warnings . . . Congress is forfeiting the chance to institute reforms that could forestall the bureaucratic crisis that continued inattention to the problem may force on us." The policies of the deposit insurance agencies, and their procedures for managing insolvencies are covered in the second chapter. The weaknesses of the insurance system are presented, including information on loss experience and risk exposure. Tables show information related to FSLIC and FDIC insolvencies. Exposure to interest risk by the insurance agencies, emerging risk, and the insurance subsidy are covered in depth. In the final chapter Mr. Kane offers six points for deposit insurance reform: market-value accounting; expanded opportunities to manage risk exposure; recalibration of insurance coverages; risk-related premiums; mixed private and government opportunities in deposit insurance; and statutory constraints to rescue large insolvent institutions.

69. Kane, Edward J. **How Incentive-Incompatible Deposit-Insurance Funds Fail**. Prochnow Report No. PR-014. Madison, WS: Prochnow Educational Foundation, 1988. 19 p.

Mr. Kane examines the failure of both the Ohio Deposit Guarantee Fund and the Maryland Savings-Share Insurance Corporation, to show a parallel with the FSLIC. He states that without reforms "a parallel meltdown by FSLIC cannot be dismissed." His examination seeks to support this statement. Sixteen pages of tables and references are included.

70. Kane, Edward J. "The Incentive Incompatibility of Government-Sponsored Deposit-Insurance Funds." In **The Reform of Federal Deposit Insurance: Disciplining the Government and Protecting Taxpayers**, pp. 144-166. Edited by James R. Barth and R. Dan Brumbaugh. [N.Y.]: HarperBusiness, 1992. 310 p. index.

The difficulties of deposit insurers are discussed in this paper. Tables show data about state insurance systems as far back as 1829. Problems with the funds are traced to incentives to misregulate, and principal-agent problems with monitoring and enforcement. The Ohio Deposit Guarantee Fund and the Maryland Savings-Share Insurance Corporation failures are discussed. Mr. Kane also discusses FSLIC and the Federal Home Loan Bank Board. He states that the FHLBB and GAO "ignored the value of the claims that capital forbearance implicitly levied against FSLIC reserves." He states, "Circumstantial evidence suggests that congressional interest in restraining FHLB regulators was at least partly rooted in a desire to sustain or repay campaign contributions." This paper provides a valuable discussion of the role deposit insurance played in the S&L crisis. References are given.

71. Kane, Edward J. "The Role of Government in the Thrift Industry's Net-worth Crisis." In **Financial Services: The Changing Institutions and Government Policy**, pp 156-184. Edited by George J. Benston. Englewood Cliffs, NJ: Prentice-Hall, Inc., 1983. 285 p. index. American Assembly, Columbia University, April 7-10, 1983.

Mr. Kane contends that the root of S&L problems is the mispricing of federal deposit insurance. He also states that the industry's, "Recurrent crises arise from . . . addiction to . . . portfolio risks." Charter conversions and public policy are also explored.

72. Kane, Edward J. "Who Should Learn What From the Failure and Delayed Bailout of the ODGF?" In **Merging Commercial and Investment Banking**, pp. 306-326. Chicago: Federal Reserve Bank of Chicago, [1988]. 630 p. Proceedings of the 23rd Annual Conference on Bank Structure and Competition, May 6-8, 1987.

The chronology of the ODGF and its resolution is reviewed. It is also outlined in chart form. The author states that he is portraying ODGF "as a small-scale version of the massively undercapitalized . . . FSLIC." Mr. Kane addresses politicians, regulators, taxpayers, and depositors with a discussion of the lessons to be learned from the ODGF failure. References are given.

73. Kaufman, George G. **Are Some Banks Too Large to Fail?: Myth and Reality**. Working Paper Series, Issues in Financial Regulation No. 89-14. Chicago: Federal Reserve Bank of Chicago, August 1989. 13 p.

The Texas S&L experience is discussed in this overview of the "too large to fail" issue. Mr. Kaufman relates that S&Ls did not match the higher interest rates offered by money market funds, and therefore experienced an outflow of funds in late 1988 - 1989. He notes this is not considered to be a run. Although depositors withdrew their money from thrifts due to concern about insolvency, the funds were generally deposited at healthier institutions. He describes this as "type-one runs-direct redeposits." He notes however, that "depositors may have avoided redepositing at healthy SLAs in Texas." The author asserts that regulators have not distinguished between disintermediation and runs in an effort to build public support for the S&L rescue proposal. He further comments that "deposit insurance has caused more frequent and greater runs to bad banks, which offered higher deposit rates, than . . . has caused runs from bad banks." The focus of this paper is a discussion of "too large to fail" as it relates to commercial banks.

74. Meigs, A. James and John C. Goodman. **Federal Deposit Insurance: The Case for Radical Reform**. NCPA Policy Report No. 155. Dallas, TX: National Center for Policy Analysis, December 1990. 25 p.

The author uses historical examples of deposit insurance failure to support his point that "no deposit insurance scheme has ever been successful over a long period of time." He lists the steps necessary to eliminate deposit insurance.

75. O'Driscoll, Gerald P., Jr. **Banking Reform**. Research Paper No. 9004. Dallas: Federal Reserve Bank of Dallas, February 1990. 30 p.

An examination of the thrift crisis and banking system problems is presented in this paper. The author also examines proposed remedies. He explains deposit insurance and its role in the debacle noting that it "is one American idea that should be discarded, not imitated." A significant portion of the paper is devoted to the topic of deposit insurance reform. References are given.

76. O'Driscoll, Gerald P., Jr. **Depository Institution Failures: The Deposit Insurance Connection**. Research Paper No. 8707. Dallas, TX : Federal Reserve Bank of Dallas, 1987. 22 p.

Mr. O'Driscoll discusses the theory that deposit insurance dictates the need for bank regulation. The author argues that "further deregulation would be stabilizing not destabilizing." The information presented in the paper is in support of this statement. The Glass-Steagall Act and its creation is reviewed. Mr. O'Driscoll discusses why it would be prudent to allow depository institutions to diversify their investments. The role of deposit insurance in the thrift crisis is described. Public policy proposals are examined in the final section of the paper. References are included.

77. **Recommendations for Change in the Federal Deposit Insurance System**. [n.p.]: The Working Group of the Cabinet Council on Economic Affairs, January 1985. 75 p. [18] p.

This paper reviews the creation of the current system, and describes the status of the insurance funds. The relevant goals of the insurance systems are described. The major options are analyzed, including privatization and changes in institutional capital. Recommendations are advanced which cover five areas: risk-related pricing, increased capital requirements, accounting, increase of size and flexibility of funds, and examination and enforcement. A review of the FDIC and FHLBB proposals are included. Numerous charts and graphs are contained in the paper.

78. Report of the Savings Association Insurance Fund Industry Advisory Committee: Executive Summary. [n.p.]: SAIF Industry Advisory Committee, July 1990. 5 p.

The report was submitted to the Committee on Banking, Finance and Urban Affairs and the Committee on Banking, Housing and Urban Affairs. The Committee urged Congress to take action to prevent further losses. The committee found that SAIF will have inadequate funds to perform its role as insurer. Their recommendations were that funds designated for SAIF not be counted as available to cover RTC losses, and that the $32 billion designated in FIRREA as contributions to SAIF be preserved. The committee commented on insurance premium parity, regulatory independence, retroactive passive loss restrictions, QTL test, and purchased mortgage servicing rights. The committee was established by FIRREA to make recommendations to the FDIC. The summary is from the June 1990 semi-annual report.

79. Restructuring the Federal Deposit Insurance System. n.p.: The Garn Institute of Finance, [1988]. [98] p. The Garn Institute of Finance Annual Conference, November 12-15, 1988, Key Largo, Florida.

The topic of this conference was "Restructuring the Federal Deposit Insurance System". The conference summary includes a copy of the statement of Frederick D. Wolf before the Committee on the Budget, U.S. Senate dated October 5, 1988, "Budgetary Implications of the Savings and Loan Crisis". A summary of the Garn Institute research on federal deposit insurance describes the two papers commissioned by the Institute. The papers were: "The Costs of Liquidating Failed Banks" by Christopher James, and "Is There a FSLIC Premium? An Analysis of Deposit Rates, Deposit Insurers, and the Risk of the Institutions" by Leonard Van Drunen and Karen Wikstrom. The 1988 academic conference is reviewed, with summaries of the sessions, and the papers presented. Included in this booklet is a copy of the "Report of the National Council of Savings Institutions Task Force on Operating Limits for Capital-Impaired Institutions", the remarks of Mark Riedy at the Western States' 1988 convention, and a statement by Charles Koch published in the American Banker, October 31, 1988. Also incorporated is a paper by Joseph Diamond and Sharon Heaton, "Structures and Considerations for Reorganizing Banks and Bank Holding Companies".

80. Shadow Financial Regulatory Committee. **Statement of the Shadow Financial Regulatory Committee on An Outline of a Program for Deposit Insurance Reform.** Statement No. 38. Chicago: Shadow Financial Regulatory Committee, December 5, 1988. 8 p.

A proposal to correct the flaws in deposit insurance, and to manage the transition to a new system, this paper specifies the steps which must be taken to accomplish the reform.

81. Thompson, A. Frank, Jr. **An Actuarial Perspective on the Adequacy of the FSLIC Fund.** Research Working Paper No. 102. Washington, D.C.: Federal Home Loan Bank Board, February 25, 1981. 47 p.

The author explores the use of actuarials to estimate possible FSLIC losses, based on models used by life and casualty companies. He notes that one advantage would be to allow insurance coverage based on the mix of deposits at each institution. He suggests that FSLIC adjust premiums semiannually to allow for variance in risk at individual institutions. The author explores various types of losses, and whether FSLIC should be responsible for those losses. He advocates a risk based premium, or alternately reducing the amount of insurance per account to reflect the amount of risk. He also questions whether the current FSLIC funds are sufficient for the coverage provided. Mr. Thompson presents recommendations for FSLIC policy. Models are included and discussed. Three pages of references follow the text.

82. Todd, Walker F. **No Conspiracy, But a Convenient Forgetting: Dr. Pangloss Visits the World of Deposit Insurance.** Washington, D.C.: Cato Institute, 1988. 46 p. Presented to a conference sponsored by the Cato Institute, November 2, 1988. 46 p.

The stated premise of this presentation is that there should be "no public subsidy of banks' risk-taking activities". The author calls for reconsideration of this, and three additional "fundamental principles" of the financial industry in discussing the insulation of banking risk from deposit insurance.

83. Vartanian, Thomas P. **A Blueprint for the Restructuring of the FSLIC.** [Washington, D.C.: Fried, Frank, Harris, Shriver & Jacobson], 1988. 16 p. The Garn Institute of Finance Annual Conference, November 12-15, 1988, Key Largo, Florida.

The FDIC and FSLIC were never intended to handle the losses with which they have been confronted. Termination of these funds and comprehensive deposit insurance reform may be in the best interest of the public. A non-partisan solution is needed. Recommendations and conclusions are presented in the paper based on five assumptions: the thrift industry and distinct regulators will be retained; failed institutions will be closed immediately; consolidation of FSLIC and FDIC agencies; utilize taxpayer funds as a last resort; and rehabilitate the system. A ten-year FSLIC plan should be developed and the resulting agency chairman should be appointed for seven years. A single agency head should be created, with employees removed from civil service, to encourage long term employment. Five regulatory changes for a separate thrift industry are presented: adoption of a risk-based deposit insurance system, risk-based capital requirements, regulation of state-chartered institutions to adjust for exercise of powers not available to federal thrifts, streamlining of ability to identify and respond to unsound activities, and establishment of a meaningful reporting system. The paper continues by outlining other points, such as curtailing the losses, allowing strong thrifts to exit FSLIC, liquidation of insolvent thrifts, and modifying the thrift franchise product by separating the workout function from the deposit and loan functions. The funding of the successor to FSLIC, which is described as FSLIC II, is discussed in detail.

84. Wells, F. Jean. **Banks and Thrifts: Restructuring and Solvency.** CRS Issue Brief IB89002. Washington, D.C.: Congressional Research Service, Library of Congress, May 5, 1989. 15 p.

A brief review of the policy issues involved in the proposals for strengthening deposit insurance funds is presented. A reading list is included.

85. Woodward, G. Thomas. **The Economics of Deposit Insurance.** CRS Report for Congress 89-32E. Washington, D.C.: Congressional Research Service, Library of Congress, January 4, 1989. 18 p.

A reassessment of deposit insurance in light of the recent cost to the economy is the goal of this paper. The benefits, costs, and economics of reform are reviewed.

REGULATORY OVERSIGHT

86. American Bankers Association. **The FSLIC Crisis: Principles and Issues A Call to Action**. Washington, D.C.: American Bankers Association, 1988. 27 p.

The ABA FSLIC Oversight Committee report discusses the issues involved in the crisis. They assert that inadequate regulation led to the insolvencies. The Committee notes that thrift institutions were technically insolvent on a market value basis by $100 billion in 1981. Forebearances were granted because it was felt that the problems would be corrected when the high interest rates modulated. The study notes, "It is in error to think that deregulation . . . caused the FSLIC's insolvency. The weakness . . . was the FHLBB's failure to strengthen its examination and supervisory policies." The Committee urges specific action, within set time frames, to resolve the crisis. They discuss the need to bring thrift regulation up to the level of commercial bank regulation. Timely liquidation of insolvent thrifts is urged, and the creation of a "liquidating trust or corporation" is suggested. The committee urges a review of housing finance incentives, and the necessity of a separate industry. Tables and charts reflecting FSLIC financial figures are included.

87. American Bankers Association. **Savings and Loan Association Regulatory Reform: Action Recommendations and Historical Perspective**. FSLIC Oversight Committee Report. Washington, D.C.: American Bankers Association, December 1987. 29 p.

One half of this paper focuses on the history of S&L regulatory weaknesses. ABA recommendations for reform are offered. Tables and graphs related to the crisis are included.

88. Balderston, Frederick E. **New Entry Into the S&L Industry, 1980-82 and Beyond.** Center for Real Estate and Urban Economics Working Paper Series No. 83-71. Berkeley, CA: University of California, 1983. 21 p.

The incentives for entry into the S&L industry were eliminated during the early 1980s due to financial instability. In late 1982 and 1983 there was an upsurge in new charter applications due to falling interest rates, and wider powers available as a result of Garn-St Germain. With the large increase in applications Mr. Balderston examines the pros and cons of regulated entry in relationship to the effect on the community and on competition.

89. Barth, James R. and Martin A. Regalia. "The Evolving Role of Regulation in the Savings and Loan Industry." In **The Financial Services Revolution: Policy Directions for the Future,** pp. 113-61. Edited by Catherine England and Thomas Huertas. Boston: Kluwer Academic Publishers, 1988. 361 p. index. Proceedings of a conference held Feb. 26-27, 1987, sponsored by the Cato Institute.

Beginning with the origin of S&Ls in 1831, this paper traces their development and the evolving role of regulation. Tables are provided with related historical data. References are included. The appendix lists major depository financial institution legislation.

90. Benston, George J. "Direct Investments and FSLIC Losses." In **Research in Financial Services: Private and Public Policy,** pp. 25-77. Edited by George G. Kaufman. Greenwich, CT: JAI Press, Inc., 1989. 262 p.

Regulations limiting direct investments is the focus of this paper. The author explores the correlation between FSLIC losses and direct investment. He conducts detailed analysis, as well as reviewing studies by other economists. His studies show that direct investments actually reduce risk. Tables, charts, and references are included.

91. Benston, George J. "The Regulation of Financial Services." In **Financial Services: The Changing Institutions and Government Policy,** pp 28-63. Edited by George J. Benston. Englewood Cliffs, NJ: Prentice-Hall, Inc., 1983. 285 p. index. American Assembly, Columbia University, April 7-10, 1983.

Historical reasons and the rationale for financial regulations are given. An assessment of the benefits and costs of regulation are included, as well as recommendations. S&L regulations are included in the discussion.

92. Benston, George J. and George G. Kaufman. **Risk and Solvency Regulation of Depository Institutions: Past Policies and Current Options.** Monograph Series in Finance and Economics 1988-1. N.Y.: Graduate School of Business Administration New York University, 1988. 89 p.

The authors present the reasons depository institutions are regulated and evaluate those reasons. They review the proposals for changing the regulatory system, and evaluate the costs and benefits of the proposals. The authors then present alternative proposals. Tables are included in the text, and references are provided. This title, with insignificant differences, was also published by the Federal Reserve Bank of Chicago as Staff Memoranda 88-1.

93. Bisenius, Donald J. **An Analysis of the Proposed Capital Requirements for Thrift Institutions: A Staff Economic Study.** Washington, D.C.: Federal Home Loan Bank Board, August 15, 1986. 185 p.

The FHLBB issued proposed capital requirements on April 24, 1986, in its efforts to limit FSLIC's risk exposure. The proposal would increase capital levels to 6% of liabilities; require growth to be capitalized at 6%; require incremental capital on direct and certain other investments; and expand components of qualifying-balances duration. This study analyzes the feasibility of the proposal. Simulation analysis suggests that: 627 institutions had capital ratios of less than 3%; 800 institutions will require external capital; new external capital needed is projected to be $20 billion if interest rates rise significantly; average industry growth would be limited to 6-9% if no new external capital is invested. The authors of the study suggested four modifications to the proposed requirements. The authors state that "the 2500 institutions with current capital-to-liability ratios above three percent should have little difficulty raising the capital needed . . . institutions with current ratios below three percent will have difficulty meeting either proposal." Also included are chapters on the effect of recapitalization on thrifts, proposed new accounting rules, and numerous tables with supporting data. Mr. Bisenius was the project coordinator, there were many contributors to the study.

94. Brumbaugh, R. Dan, Jr. **Thrifts Under Siege: Restoring Order to American Banking.** Cambridge, MA: Ballinger Publishing Co., 1988. 214 p. index.

A former FHLBB chief economist, Mr. Brumbaugh, presents a detailed analysis of the thrift crisis. He discusses the two crises between 1980 and 1987, and shows how regulatory response to the early problems created the later crisis. He asserts that reform of deposit insurance is not necessary, but urges early closing of insolvent thrifts and reliance on market-value net worth. The author recommends changes to the regulatory structure, including consolidation of thrift and bank regulation. Included are supporting tables and references.

95. Bryan, Lowell L. **Breaking Up the Bank: Rethinking an Industry Under Siege**. Homewood, IL: Dow Jones-Irwin, 1988. 209 p. index.

In the early 1970s large depositors and high-quality borrowers began to migrate from banks to services offered by securities firms. With the introduction of competition into the system it is now necessary to design a banking system that is not founded "on protective regulation and cross-subsidies, but on providing fair value to each customer." The author points out that deposit insurance combined with competition will lead to high costs of various types. He advocates a new regulatory framework instead of reregulation. Also advocated is a new management model built on structured securitized credit. Throughout the text references are made to both banks and thrifts, relating to deposit insurance, lending, regulatory agencies, and management decisions. One portion of a chapter discusses the future of thrifts and the cost to FSLIC. Another sub-chapter discusses thrift regulatory inadequacy. Regarding thrift insolvencies he states, "our best estimate is that it is already taking some $7 to $10 billion per year of new cash to keep the existing system from collapsing on itself, excluding any of the money needed for direct cash infusions from the FSLIC." While thrifts play a small role in the topic of this book, the discussion shows how thrifts fit into the overall view of financial institutions. The future of financial institutions as seen through the author's presentation may be of interest to those studying our financial system. A bibliography is included.

96. **Capital Adequacy for Banks and Thrifts**. Commercial Law and Practice Course Handbook Series No. 414. [New York]: Practising Law Institute, 1987. 680 p.

This collection is composed of a combination of short and detailed outlines. The detailed outlines provide useful information. Ira L. Tannenbaum's presentation, "Overview of Methods for Thrifts to Generate Regulatory Capital", discusses the Bank Board's regulatory capital requirement to become effective January 1, 1987. Basic capital requirements of FSLIC insured institutions were to increase to 6% of total liabilities over a multi-year transition period. Mr. Tannenbaum's presentation provides an overview of the regulatory focus on ways in which institutions can raise regulatory capital from sources other than retained earnings. This section contains tables listing "completed or announced acquisition conversions", and "completed modified conversions". Julie L. Williams' paper was on the same subject, "Overview of the FHLBB's Regulatory Capital Requirements". Her paper covers the liability and contingency component, maturity matching credit, and the special treatment of

De Novo and "certain other" S&Ls. Included in this topic was the application of the "growth rule" and enforcement of supervisory procedures as contained in SP-62.

97. Carron, Andrew S. **The Plight of the Thrift Institutions**. Studies in the regulation of economic activity series. Washington, D.C.: The Brookings Institution, 1982. 96 p. index.

Mr. Carron is credited with being the first to document the thrift industry's market value net worth as being devastated by the high nominal rates of 1979 and 1980. His two early works are probably the most referenced titles on the crisis. In this title he reviews the history of regulation. When ceilings on deposit interest rates were first applied in 1966 the system began to change. The industry did well until interest rates rose in the late 1970s, which weakened the industry. In this section charts reflect the profitability of thrift institutions from 1961-1981; operating expense performance 1951-1980; inflation and selected interest rates 1961-1980; market value calculations; and cash flow analysis. The figures show "that the thrift industry may be technically insolvent". The author also states, "If thrift institutions avoid a liquidity crisis, it will be at the expense of the housing industry . . . An emphasis on new programs to improve liquidity may be viewed as policy for the housing industry rather than as a means of preventing thrift institutions failures." The outlook for the thrift industry composes the second chapter of this book. Mutual savings banks are seen to be healthier than S&Ls. Various options are reviewed as transition policies which would be needed during deregulation phase-in. Policy alternatives addressing the industry problems are discussed. The alternatives are presented in five categories: direct assistance, regulatory policy, tax law, direct lending, and secondary market activities. The author concludes by stating that the industry must be allowed to adjust to market conditions.

98. Carron, Andrew S. "The Political Economy of Financial Regulation." In **The Political Economy of Deregulation: Interest Groups in the Regulatory Process**, pp. 69-83. By Roger G. Noll and Bruce M. Owen. Washington, D.C.: American Enterprise Institute for Public Policy Research, 1983. 164 p.

Mr. Carron discusses three major regulations, and how rules can create and maintain preferences that may not be in broad public interest. The regulations are: rate ceilings, limitations on investment powers of S&Ls, and restrictions on bank powers. Rate controls were intended to promote housing by making it possible for cheaper mortgages to be offered. Mr. Carron says, "there is scant evidence that the low-cost deposits were ever passed through to mortgage borrowers." He states that savings institutions did receive higher profits due to rate controls. Interest groups lobbied to continue the favored positions of thrifts. In exchange for removal of many regulatory restrictions the industry acquiesced to a relaxation of rate controls. Limited new asset powers for thrifts were granted in 1980. Commercial lending powers were granted in 1982. The author concludes by pointing out that regulations must adapt to changing conditions. Regulations intended for safety and soundness now serve private interests.

99. **Current Issues in the Financial Services Industries**. New York: Ernst & Young, October 1989. 137 p.

This annual publication summarizes emerging issues and regulatory positions that affect the industry. Five major categories are included: legislative and regulatory, capital markets, foreign loans, asset quality, and reporting. The legislative and regulatory section covers thrifts, banks, and investment companies. Earlier editions were titled **Current Issues: Banks and Thrift Institutions**, while a later edition's title was **Current Issues for Depository Institutions**. The topics covered vary with the year's events.

100. Doyle, A. Patrick. "Capital Adequacy for Banks and Thrifts: New Regulations and Financing Techniques." In **Capital Adequacy for Banks and Thrifts: New Regulations and Financing Techniques**, pp.541-728. New York: Practising Law Institute, 1985. 735 p. Commercial Law and Practice Course Handbook Series No. 358. Prepared for distribution at the Capital Adequacy for Banks and Thrifts: New Regulations and Financing Techniques Program, July 18-19, 1985, New York City.

This section includes several FHLBB regulations in their entirety. Included are: Net Worth Regulation; Mutual to Stock Regulations; Issuance of Subordinated Debt Securities; Accounting Requirements; Borrowing Limitations; Earnings Based Account Regulation; and the Finance Subsidiaries Regulation. Three recent court cases of interest are discussed: Marine Bank vs. Weaver, Wolf v. Banco Nacional de Mexico, S.A., and Gary Plastic Packaging Corp. v. Merrill Lynch, Pierce, Fenner & Smith, Inc..

101. Eisenbeis, Robert A. "New Investment Powers: Diversification or Specialization." In **Strategic Planning for Economic and Technological Change in the Financial Services Industry**, pp. 107-121. San Francisco, CA: Federal Home Loan Bank of San Francisco, 1983. 179 p. Proceedings of the Eighth Annual Conference, December 9-10, 1982.

Portfolio diversification was advocated by the FINE Study, and later, in 1971 by the Hunt Commission. It was not until 1980, with DIDMCA, that expanded diversification for S&Ls was possible. The 1982 Garn-St Germain Act provided significant portfolio diversification features. This paper reviews the "problem" S&Ls face in deciding to completely diversify, or to remain specialized mortgage lenders. It examines how state-chartered thrifts with broadened powers have performed, and discusses research on the performance of commercial banks specializing in real estate lending. The changes in asset and liability powers of S&Ls is discussed, and a table summarizes the changes. The author concludes "the possibility exists" that S&Ls can remain specialized mortgage lenders and also be profitable. References are included.

102. England, Catherine. "A Market Approach to the Savings and Loan Crisis." In **An American Vision: Policies for the '90s**, pp. 105-128. Edited by Edward H. Crane and David Boaz. Washington, D.C.: Cato Institute, 1989. 358 p.

Ms. England reviews the regulatory constraints on financial institutions. She makes detailed recommendations for reforms which are needed to allow financial institutions to move forward into the future.

103. Fain, Thomas A. **Interest Rate Risk Measurement and TB-13**. Chicago: Financial Managers Society, Inc., 1989. 37 p.

Thrift Bulletin 13 on interest rate risk was issued on January 26, 1989, by the Federal Home Loan Bank System's Office of Regulatory Activities. This publication covers methods of complying with the regulation, and how to implement interest rate risk management. The paper begins with a discussion of interest rate risk. The chapter on measurement techniques includes gap and duration analysis. The last section is a step-by-step guide to measuring institution sensitivity. A checklist for developing a policy statement is provided.

104. **First Annual Regulatory Developments in the Savings and Loan Industry**. New York: Law Journal Seminars-Press, Inc., 1980. 454 p.

The materials in this collection are primarily in outline form; however, some are lengthy enough to be useful. Several papers are on the subject of equity financing for S&Ls, i.e. Richard Kneipper's paper on "Debt and Pass-Through Offerings". Mergers, acquisitions, and defending against takeovers are additional subjects covered in this material. The remainder of the papers presented cover "new powers" and "new environments" for S&Ls.

105. Garcia, Gillian. "The FSLIC is 'Broke' in More Ways Than One." In **The Financial Services Revolution: Policy Directions for the Future**, pp. 234-49. Edited by Catherine England and Thomas Huertas. Boston: Kluwer

Academic Publishers, 1988. 361 p. index. Proceedings of a conference held
Feb. 26-27, 1987, sponsored by the Cato Institute.

Regulatory error is the focus of this paper. The author argues that allowing
large numbers of insolvent institutions to continue operating is the most crucial
error, and threatens the viability of the entire industry. Resolution options and
S&L risk taking are reviewed. Related tables and references are included.

106. Gart, Alan. **Banks, Thrifts, and Insurance Companies.** Lexington,
MA: Lexington Books, 1985. 136 p. index.

Regulation and deregulation is surveyed. The DIDMCA and the Garn-St
Germain Act are examined. The DIDMCA gradually phased out interest rate
ceilings, and broadened asset powers for thrifts. The author notes that Congress
did not "consider carefully enough" the effects on mortgage interest rates of the
rate ceiling elimination. Garn-St Germain was intended to allow depository
institutions to compete with money market funds. Thrifts were also given the
right to make commercial loans and accept demand deposits. A chart provides
key dates in the phase-out of Regulation Q. Technological changes such as
electronic funds transfer systems, debit cards, home banking, and videotex are
reviewed. The trend toward financial conglomerates is also examined. The
problems and solutions of the thrift industry are discussed including comments
on restructuring, adjustable-rate mortgages, asset/liability management,
conversions, swaps, hedging and futures, and accounting methods. The author
ends by presenting his view of what the coming decade holds for the industry.

107. Goldstein, Steven J. and Eric I. Hemel. **Gap Analysis: Using Section
H of the Quarterly Report.** Washington, D.C.: Federal Home Loan Bank
Board, July 1984. 17 p. [5] p.

The Bank Board introduced a quarterly reporting system to begin in 1984. The
new reports included information on the terms to maturity of a wide range of
assets and liabilities. This allowed the Bank Board to gather information on
interest-rate-risk positions. It also ensured that institution managers and
directors would have the information needed to measure their interest-rate-risk
positions. An explanation of the new information required for Section H is
given. The remainder of the paper deals with explanations related to gap
management, its short comings, and business strategies. Samples are included.

108. Greenbaum, Stuart I. "Deregulation of the Thrift Industry: A Prologue
to Transitional Problems and Risks." In **Financial Stability of the Thrift
Industry**, pp. 15-39. San Francisco: Federal Home Loan Bank of San

Francisco, 1986. 230 p. Proceedings of the Eleventh Annual Conference, December 12-13, 1985.

Approximately 1000 S&Ls disappeared between 1978-1983; the state of the industry is discussed in the beginning of the paper. The role of regulation in the evolving industry is explored, with a call to restructure the regulatory system. Specifically, the author calls for an organizational audit of the FHLB System. Further, he advocates easing conversions and mergers, increasing compensation for directors and managers, and endorses the Management Consignment Program as being constructive.

109. Hemel, Eric I., Lisa R. Wolfson, and Carol F. Garfein. **The FHLBB Maturity Matching Credit: Strategies for a New Era of Regulation.** New York: The First Boston Corporation, November 1986. 16 p.

The FHLBB finalized its minimum capital requirement rules on August 15, 1986. The regulation provides a "maturity matching credit" against minimum capital requirements. The institution's interest rate risk exposure will determine the credit. The credit allows thrifts to reduce their minimum capital requirements by up to two percentage points. The new regulation "allows savings institutions with sufficiently small maturity mismatches to reduce overall minimum capital requirements to as low as 3% prior to 1990 and 4% thereafter." This paper discusses the mechanics of the credit, how the maturity mismatches will be measured, and strategies thrifts might use to reduce interest rate risk and maximize the credit available to them. Techniques discussed in the paper are adjustable rate mortgages, asset portfolio restructuring, long-term liabilities, and hedging strategies,

110. Horvitz, Paul M. and R. Richardson Pettit. "Short-Run Financial Solutions for Troubled Thrift Institutions." In **The Future of the Thrift Industry,** pp. 44-67. Conference Series No. 24. Boston: Federal Reserve Bank of Boston, [1982]. 187 p. Proceedings of a Conference held October 1981.

The authors argue that "some regulatory adjustment or form of aid to the industry" is justified because of regulatory policies and economics which contributed to the thrift industry's financial difficulties. Specific contributors are regulations prohibiting diversification, interest rate increases, and the cost of allowing failure when there may be a chance of long-run viability. The costs, benefits, and potential for success of various plans to help thrifts "bridge the gap" are discussed in this paper. A detailed discussion of bankruptcy is presented. The authors conclude by reflecting that it will be necessary to determine which institutions have a chance for survival, noting that those that do not have a chance will take unusual risks. They state that most well-run institutions can be profitable, and that it is in the best interest of the insurance fund to keep these institutions viable. The authors' preference is for a direct injection of funds at a zero or low interest rate, with structuring to allow the agency to recoup some of the benefits from success.

111.   Huertas, Thomas F.   "The Regulation of Financial Institutions: A Historical Perspective on Current Issues." In **Financial Services: The Changing Institutions and Government Policy**, pp 6-27. Edited by George J. Benston. Englewood Cliffs, NJ: Prentice-Hall, Inc., 1983. 285 p. index. American Assembly, Columbia University, April 7-10, 1983.

Glass-Steagall is included in the regulatory review which begins with banking in 1791 and touches on various regulations throughout the years. The paper briefly touches on S&L history.

112.   Kane, Edward J.   "Defective Regulatory Incentives and the Bush Initiative." In **Restructuring the American Financial System**, pp. 117-127. Edited by George G. Kaufman. Boston: Kluwer Academic Publishers, 1990. 180 p. index.

A footnote indicates that this paper extends Kane's 1989 work, *The S&L Insurance Mess: How Did It Happen?*, published by The Urban Institute Press. Mr. Kane states that FIRREA is not based on a "complete theory of how the mess happened" and therefore it "construes the problem too narrowly and too wishfully." He continues by stating that the roots of the problems are "in the aggravation of losses associated initially with adverse economic developments by longstanding defects in political and bureaucratic accountability for federal financial regulation." Mr. Kane discusses the lack of government action to deal with the S&L problems, the "delaying tactics" of the FHLBB, and the "dangerous regulatory propensities". The four propensities are: keeping themselves uninformed; using the weight of the office to reassure doubters; concealing past mistakes; and looking for scapegoats. The author concludes his paper by presenting recommendations to improve "incentives for politicians and regulators". A short list of references are included.

113. Kaplan, Donald M. "Alternative Strategies for Success." In **The Future of the Thrift Industry**, pp. 81-105. San Francisco: Federal Home Loan Bank of San Francisco, 1989.   253 p. Proceedings of the Fourteenth Annual Conference, December 8-9, 1988.

Eight distinct operating strategies and the performance of thrifts using each strategy are examined. A sample of 2,087 institutions were used in the analysis, as of June 30, 1988. Only institutions more than five years old with positive net worth were included. The strategy groups studied were: single-family, multifamily, commercial, real estate/ADC, wholesale, consumer bank, mortgage banking, and diversified. For half the sample "the primary product line strategy continues to be single-family residential mortgage lending." The analysis indicates "that capital ratios may well have as much or more of an impact on the success of a thrift than the strategies pursued." The results support risk-based capital regulations. Eighteen tables present supporting data.

114. Litan, Robert E. "The American Banking System: Dangers and Tasks Ahead." In **Economic Vulnerabilities: Challenges for Policymakers**, pp. 34-54. Edited by Susan Irving. Washington, D.C.: Curry Foundation, [1988]. 86 p. A policy study by the Curry Foundation.

Mr. Litan discusses the problems inherent in bank and thrift powers, and the flaw in deposit insurance. The author calls for a speedy resolution to the thrift crisis to prevent impact on the economy. He lists six steps for reform.

115. Maris, Brian A. **Savings and Loans and Consumer Credit: An Assessment.** Research Working Paper No. 94. Washington, D.C.: Federal Home Loan Bank Board, April 1980. 75 p.

An assessment was made regarding the possible impact on the industry of consumer credit lending because legislation was pending which would allow thrifts this new power. The author analyzes the rate on consumer credit as compared with mortgage lending. He also explores the ability of lenders to control the volume of consumer credit, and the potential for issuing credit cards. Mr. Maris projects the impact of consumer lending on S&L earnings. His analysis shows that consumer lending will not have a measurable impact on the average rate of return on assets. However, short term lending may reduce the instability of S&L earnings. Consumer lending will also help in the competition for deposits. The author concludes by stating that "consumer lending will be neither the salvation nor the death knell of S&Ls." Extensive references are included.

116. Martin, Preston. "Savings Banking in the Next Decade." In **Financial Stability of the Thrift Industry**, pp. 5-11. San Francisco: Federal Home Loan Bank of San Francisco, 1986. 230 p. Proceedings of the Eleventh Annual Conference, December 12-13, 1985.

Mr. Martin, Chairman of the FHLBB from 1969-1982, advocates self-regulation for the industry to overcome its problems. He points out that "regulations are often poorly designed and administered." But the move to deregulation requires some oversight. Other industries exercise self-regulation, which he feels could successfully be applied to thrifts. Specifically mentioned are standards for good business practices, code of ethics, accreditation standards, model strategic plans, and surveillance procedures. To avoid reregulation the industry should take charge of its future by forming an industry commission to institute self-regulation.

117.   Murphy, M. Maureen. **Powers of Federally Chartered Thrifts Compared With Those of Thrifts Chartered by Various States**. CRS Report for Congress 89-171A. Washington, D.C.: Congressional Research Service, March 14, 1989. 6 p.

State chartered thrifts are compared with federally chartered thrifts for selected states. An examination was made of statues for the states of California, Colorado, Connecticut, Florida, and Texas, which revealed a wide range of powers not permitted to federal thrifts.

118.   **1984 Task Force on Broader Earnings Opportunities for Savings Institutions**. Chicago: United States League of Savings Institutions, 1984. 30 p.

In the environment of increased competition the task force was formed to focus on strategies to restore profitability to the savings institution business. An overview of the need for and barriers to broader earnings opportunities is given. The report stresses insuring parity for federally chartered institutions with state-chartered institutions, and the need for expanded investments in service corporations. The task force recommended: S&Ls be market-driven; use of real estate expertise as basis for expansion; overcome barriers, i.e. overregulation and changes in accounting rules; improve operating efficiencies; require regulatory changes to achieve parity; and an increase of resources allocated by the U.S. League to develop profitable activities for S&Ls.

119.   Olin, Harold. "The Thrift Institutions' Experience With Service Corporations." In **Merging Commercial and Investment Banking**, pp. 101-117. Chicago: Federal Reserve Bank of Chicago, [1988]. 630 p. Proceedings of the 23rd Annual Conference on Bank Structure and Competition, May 6-8, 1987.

Service corporations have served as a vehicle to allow thrifts to diversify their investments. The regulations list 40-50 separate activities which thrifts can do through service corporations. Federally chartered institutions are limited to investing a maximum of 3% in service corporation activities. State chartered institution powers are diverse. Tables in the text show investment limits in each of the 50 states for federal and state chartered institutions. A second table shows equity risk investment and capital requirements. The author points out the opportunities available to thrifts to "produce fee income from non-traditional investments and activities."

120. Ornstein, Franklin H. **Savings Banking an Industry in Change.** Reston, VA: Reston Publishing Co., 1985. 331 p.

The development of the savings industry, its history, and the government actions which have shaped it are the topics of this book. The author points out, that for almost 200 years, savings institutions operated without significant changes until the DIDMCA of 1980 provided extensive new powers. The majority of the book is devoted to examining regulatory developments. A long discussion of conversions explained, "New injections of capital via stock issues would potentially provide a source of capital in capital deficit areas." Also presented are discussions of capital adequacy and supervisory mergers. Distressed associations are discussed, with a review of warehousing and various "bailout plans". FSLIC's authority to create income capital certificates and promissory notes are explained. In reviewing the industry Mr. Ornstein discusses merger policy, accounting, and taxation. He comments on the future direction of the industry. A bibliography is provided.

121. Phillips, Almarin and Donald P. Jacobs. "Reflections on the Hunt Commission." In **Financial Services: The Changing Institutions and Government Policy**, pp 235-265. Edited by George J. Benston. Englewood Cliffs, NJ: Prentice-Hall, Inc., 1983. 285 p. index. American Assembly, Columbia University, April 7-10, 1983.

The Hunt Commission was formed in June 1970 to develop recommendations for regulatory reform for deposit financial institutions. This paper reviews the resistance to reform legislation. Resistance from thrifts, real estate interests, and regulators are described. The author also evaluates the cost of the failure to deregulate.

122. Riordan, Dale. "Deregulation and the Future of the Thrift Industry." In **The Savings and Loan Industry in the 1980s**, pp. [25-43]. Research Working Paper No. 100. Washington, D.C.: Federal Home Loan Bank Board, December 1980. [43] p.

Mr. Riordan was director of the Office of Policy and Economic Research when he presented this paper at the 63rd Annual Convention of the Arkansas Savings and Loan League in September 1980. The speech relates to deregulation and the future of the industry. Mr. Riordan presents specific regulatory changes which are proposed or in the planning stages. He discusses the proposed net worth regulations, new empowerments, and outside borrowing authority. He also warns of the possible ill effects of deregulation stating that, "Deregulation means not being afraid to let marginal institutions fail. But it also means that aggressive institutions will succeed."

123. Schilling, William J. "Capital Adequacy for Banks and Thrifts." In **Capital Adequacy for Banks and Thrifts: New Regulations and Financing Techniques**, pp.261-371. New York: Practising Law Institute, 1985. 735 p. Commercial Law and Practice Course Handbook Series No. 358. Prepared for distribution at the Capital Adequacy for Banks and Thrifts: New Regulations and Financing Techniques Program, July 18-19, 1985, New York City.

The materials included in this section of the handbook relate to thrifts. The first item is a reproduction of the statement of Edwin J. Gray before the Subcommittee on Commerce, Consumer and Monetary Affairs of the Committee on Government Operations, U.S. House of Representatives 2-27-85. This is followed by the text of a presentation by William Schilling to the FHLBB Office of Examinations and Supervision District Directors on the topic of net worth and direct investment regulations dated 1-31-85. His presentation touches on four areas of management problems that the examination staff must deal with, and speaks to criticism of the new regulation. An overview of the net worth regulation is given by Robert Monheit, who is with the FHLBB Office of General Counsel. This is followed by the brokered deposit limitation final rule. The following two final rules included are amendments relating to the issuance and use of subordinated debt securities, and assets qualifying for the deferral and amortization of gains and losses. A memo to all FHLB presidents from the FHLBB on the subject of "FSLIC Criteria-Uninsured Associations", discusses the standards for conversion to FSLIC by non-federally insured depositories. The last item included in this section is the minimum net worth calculation for use in 1985.

124. Silverberg, Stanley C. **The Savings and Loan Problem in the United States**. Policy, Research, and External Affairs Working Papers # 351. Washington, D.C.: The World Bank, March 1990. 53 p.

Written from the perspective of the lessons other countries, especially developing countries, may learn from the thrift debacle this paper reviews the crisis. The author notes that the experience of deregulation accompanied by widespread losses parallels financial experiences elsewhere. After providing background on the development of the problems, Mr. Silverberg discusses the regulatory efforts to "shore up" the industry. He states that in 1981, "When the FHLBB and Congress were unwilling to acknowledge the extent of the problem, it became necessary to find ways to deal with the S&L problem that did not involve cash outlays or obvious commitments from FSLIC." He describes the development of net worth certificates, deferred losses on asset sales, and acquiring institutions being granted favorable accounting treatment. Other means to "buy time" were reducing net worth requirements, and liberalizing powers. The regulatory policies for handling failed thrifts is discussed, i.e. the FHLBB merging insolvent S&Ls into "Phoenixes" to avoid FSLIC costs. Later thrifts were placed into the "management consignment program" to avoid liquidation until the institution could be sold. Mr. Silverberg does note that some of the FSLIC tactics "probably reduced costs without creating other problems." While some "shifted costs from one pocket of government to another." Included is a discussion of the FDIC's handling of similar problems with mutual savings banks. Several pages are devoted to a discussion of FIRREA, its implementation, and effect on the industry. Mr. Silverberg concludes by discussing the effect of public policy decisions on the S&L problem. He acknowledges the combination of economic events and government policies which created the debacle. A bibliography is included in the paper.

125. Sinkley, Joseph F., Jr. "Can Regulation and Supervision Ensure Financial Stability?" In **Financial Stability of the Thrift Industry**, pp. 133-148. San Francisco: Federal Home Loan Bank of San Francisco, 1986. 230 p. Proceedings of the Eleventh Annual Conference, December 12-13, 1985.

The regulatory, supervisory, and insurance problems faced by the thrift industry are analyzed. A framework for investigating risk exposure is presented with four dimensions: subsidiary risk, portfolio risk, business risk, and regulatory and insurance risk. The paper suggests a seven-point reform package consisting of: market-value accounting; risk-based capital requirements; self-regulation; rational pricing of deposit insurance; a flexible enforcement policy; improvement of regulatory staff; and avoidance of reregulation. References are given.

126. Sirmans, G. Stacy. **Deriving a Thrift Institution's Efficient Frontiers in Constrained and Unconstrained Environments.** Research Working Paper No. 119. Washington, D.C.: Federal Home Loan Bank Board, May 1985. 24 p.

Restrictions on direct investments are explored as they would affect an institution's portfolio. "Efficient portfolios" are studied under no restrictions, a 10% maximum allowance, and no direct investments allowed. The assets included are: real estate, fixed-rate mortgages, adjustable-rate mortgages, commercial loans, and common stock. The results show that, with a 10% limitation, thrifts would have operated in a "lower-risk environment."

127. **Special Report on Thrift Regulatory Activities Guidelines.** n.p.:
Mortgage Commentary Publications, 1988. 136 p.

The forward to this report states that it "is aimed at providing some additional
perspective on many of the critical areas of regulation and compliance facing
thrifts today." It was written in response to the new handbook for supervisory
personnel issued by the Federal Home Loan Bank Board. The handbook "walks
examiners and other supervisory personnel through virtually every possible red
flag area for thrift institution managers and their boards of directors." This
report interprets and comments on the guidelines. It points out that "a message
has been sent in the handbook" relating to board of directors' involvement, risk-
taking areas such as mortgage securities and derivative products, real estate
owned, and debt restructurings. Other areas covered are asset classification,
interest rate risk management, capital adequacy, capital forbearance,
fraud/insider   abuse,   loan   portfolio   diversification,   lending,   internal
controls/audits, and present value analysis. The report presents the highlights
of each topic, and mentions the areas in which examiners are alerted to specific
action. Also noted are other documents which would be useful to institutions.
This is a concise review of the "mammoth" handbook issued by the Office of
Regulatory Affairs.

128. Strunk, Norman and Fred Case. **Where Deregulation Went Wrong: A
Look at the Causes Behind Savings and Loan Failures in the 1980's.**
Chicago : United States League of Savings Institutions, 1988. 210 p.

This study was commissioned by the U.S. League of Savings Institutions. The
prevailing theme is that the failures are the "legacy of deregulation". Four
chapters focus on historical background, the forces leading to the failures; five
chapters explore the causes of the crisis. The net worth problem, expanded
powers, and deregulation are discussed in detail. The investment powers
available to state-chartered institutions are listed for Arizona, California,
Florida, and Texas. The examination and supervision functions are extensively
reviewed. Charts and tables are used to present financial information, such as
number of failed thrifts and their assets by FHLB district, and by state. The
addenda include reproductions of articles, a net worth index, and a cease and
desist order.

129. Thompson, A. Frank, Jr., Linda E. Bowyer, and A. Bhattacharya.
**Theoretical Propositions on the Effect Minimum Net Worth Requirements
Have on Insolvency and Bankruptcy for Stock Savings and Loan
Associations.** Invited Research Working Paper No. 51. Washington, D.C.:
Federal Home Loan Bank Board, March 14, 1985. 11 p.

The relationship between net worth requirements and the likelihood of insolvency for stock S&Ls is explored in this study. A dynamic model, based on Jorg Finsinger's 1983 formulation for insurance companies, illustrates how dividend policy and capital values are inter-related for stock S&Ls. References are given.

130. **Thrift Acquisitions and Supervisory Problems: The F.D.I.C. & F.H.L.B.B. Speak.** New York: Law & Business, Inc., 1982. 602 p.

This title is a compilation of various papers and other documents. Among the papers included is a presentation by the Director of FSLIC, H. Brent Beesley on "FSLIC: Yesterday, Today and Tomorrow". A series of materials related to income capital certificates: summary of principal provisions of certificates to be issued by a mutual S&L to FSLIC, sample master agreement, five year promissory note, and purchase agreement are incorporated. Two papers by Thomas Vartanian are included, "Supervisory Solutions: The Need for Innovations and Modernization, An Outline" and "The Role of Savings and Loan Holding Companies in the Current Regulatory Climate". Several items relating to bank acquisitions of mutual savings banks are reproduced in this material. Two papers relating to bank holding company acquisitions of thrifts, and a paper on tax and accounting aspects of supervisory S&Ls are in this collection.

131. **The Thrift Institutions Restructuring Act of 1981: A Staff Economic Analysis.** Washington, D.C.: Federal Home Loan Bank Board, October 1981. 121 p.

The Act proposed structural changes for the thrift industry among which were wider investment authority, ability to shorten the average asset maturity, and new services. Also included were due-on-sale provisions, and FSLIC powers to deal with failing thrifts. The study simulated various aspects of the Act using balance sheets and income statements projected from 1981-1986. The conclusion was that the Act would allow thrifts to reduce profit volatility which would reduce the need for future FSLIC assistance. Ninety-four pages of projections are included in the analysis. Senator Garn introduces the Act as S.1703.

132. Tuccillo, John A., David J. Hartzell and Stephen J. Malpezzi. **The Competition Between Savings and Loan Associations and Money Market Mutual Funds: Empirical Estimates and Technical Issues.** Washington, D.C.: The Urban Institute, May 1981. 75 p.

The competition faced by S&Ls for short-term deposit funds from Money Market Mutual Funds (MMMF) is the focus of this paper. In addition to paying high returns on investments, they also offer services not available from S&Ls, i.e. funds transfer and portfolio management. If the growth of MMMFs is because institutions have been unable to pay market interest rates to small investors, then the funds should be less of a problem to S&Ls with the phase out of Regulation Q. A second theory suggests that the MMMF has grown out of a technological revolution. If this is the case S&Ls "must differentiate themselves significantly from MMMFs in order to compete effectively." The authors explore whether or not S&Ls can effectively compete with MMMFs, and if this competition will adversely impact mortgage lending. The model and results of the study are included in the paper. The conclusion is that these instruments will complement S&L services over the long term, and that the instruments can be collateralized by a pool of variable rate assets. A chapter is devoted to changes in the financial system including strategies that institutions must adopt to compete. A short bibliography is listed.

133.   Vartanian, Thomas P.   **Officer and Director Responsibilities and Liabilities: Running the Gauntlet in 1985**. Washington, D.C.: Fried, Frank, Harris, Shriver & Kampelman, [1984]. 18 p. The United States League of Savings Institutions Annual Convention, Washington, D.C., October 28, 1984.

Mr. Vartanian delivered the message that FSLIC activity was increasing related to administrative, civil and criminal actions. In fact, Congress was encouraging increased levels. "Since 1980, supervisory agreements issued by the FHLBB have increased ten fold, while formal cease-and-desist and removal and suspension orders have increased 17 and 22 times respectively." Mr. Vartanian continues by discussing various enforcement actions. He points out that officers and directors should be concerned with cases which may be brought by FSLIC as receiver "standing in the shoes of stockholders of a failed institution." He outlines what should be included in a compliance program, and encourages proper analysis and review to limit exposures for officers and directors.

134.   Vartanian, Thomas P.   "Selected Effects of the FHLBB's Direct Investment and Net Worth Regulations: Positioning for Deposit Insurance Reform."   In **Capital Adequacy for Banks and Thrifts: New Regulations and Financing Techniques**, pp.521-526. New York: Practising Law Institute, 1985. 735 p. Commercial Law and Practice Course Handbook Series No. 358. Prepared for distribution at the Capital Adequacy for Banks and Thrifts: New Regulations and Financing Techniques Program, July 18-19, 1985, New York City.

Mr. Vartanian points out that regulations must be read as closely for what is not said as what is said. He views the net worth regulation changes as encouragement for weak institutions to merge with stronger ones. The direct investment regulations are written to protect FSLIC. The author discusses the subtleties of both of these regulations. He predicts that the regulations will stimulate a Congressional review of deposit insurance. He also asserts that the bank and thrift industry will be compelled to "support the least offensive congressional solution put forward over the next few years."

135. Vartanian, Thomas P. "SIA Decision Gives a Boost to Thrift Subsidiary Powers." In **Capital Adequacy for Banks and Thrifts: New Regulations and Financing Techniques**, pp.533-540. New York: Practising Law Institute, 1985. 735 p. Commercial Law and Practice Course Handbook Series No. 358. Prepared for distribution at the Capital Adequacy for Banks and Thrifts: New Regulations and Financing Techniques Program, July 18-19, 1985, New York City.

A review of the May 9, 1984 decision in Securities Industries Association v. Federal Home Loan Bank Board is given in this reprint from **Legal Times**, July 2, 1984. The district court affirmed the FHLBB decision to allow subsidiaries of federal S&Ls to engage in the discount brokerage business. Mr. Vartanian points out that the importance of this decision is the affirmation that the FHLBB has the authority to ensure that the S&L industry is able to compete in a competitive environment.

136. Vergrugge, James A. and Robert R. Dince, Jr. "Alternative Sources of Equity Capital for Savings and Loan Associations." In **New Sources of Capital for the Savings and Loan Industry**, pp. 59-89. San Francisco: Federal Home Loan Bank of San Francisco, [1980]. 263 p. Proceedings of the Fifth Annual Conference held December 6-7, 1979.

Capital requirements have been under review as S&L net worth ratios have declined. Of importance is the function of capital and the appropriate level, and how risk relates to capital. This paper evaluates the alternative sources of equity capital for S&Ls. The industry capital situation is presented, and charts are included. Internal and external solutions are explored, i.e. sale of stock, subordinated debentures, lowered taxes, and investment authority. It suggests that the FSLIC funds be used as a source of net worth for the industry. The authors further state that, "an asset-based net worth requirement based on risk", should be mandated.

137. Wang, George H.K., Daniel Sauerhaft, and Donald Edwards. **Predicting Thrift-Institution Examination Ratings**. Research Working Paper No. 131. Washington, D.C.: Federal Home Loan Bank Board, June 1987. 60 p.

A statistical model using financial report data to predict examination ratings would aid examination staff. The purpose of this paper is to build such a model. The unique aspects of the study are that interest-rate risk/interest-sensitive funds are compared with hedged one-year gap to determine which measure receives greater examination attention. Secondly, national as well as regional models are used. The authors note that regional models out-perform national models. The model and statistical techniques used are included, and the empirical results of the models are presented. The authors state that the model can help the Bank Board create and monitor a list of potential problem thrifts, and the ratings could be used for risk-based deposit insurance. They conclude that "tangible net worth is a slightly better predictor for . . . ratings than regulatory net worth," and that "the interest-rate-sensitive fund variable can capture the examiner's concept of interest-rate risk better than the one-year hedged gap measure." References are included.

138. White, Lawrence J. **The Debacle of the S&Ls in the United States: Some Cautionary Lessons for the Regulation of Financial Institutions.** Salomon Brothers Center for the Study of Financial Institutions Working Paper Series S-90-25. New York: New York University, 1990. 25 p. [8] p.

The important lessons from the debacle are presented in this paper. A brief history of the crisis is given, with a review of S&L safety and soundness regulations and related accounting concepts. Three of the seven lessons from the crisis are: accounting must be based on market value concepts, capital standards must be based on market value accounting, and deposit insurance premiums must be risk based. He argues that fundamental regulatory reforms are vital to avoid the recurrence of the debacle. A bibliography is included in the paper.

139. Woolridge, J. Randall and Austin J. Jaffee. **Asset Diversification Strategies for Federally Chartered Savings and Loan Associations.** Research Paper No. 140. Washington, D.C.: Federal Home Loan Bank Board, April 1988. 37 p.

The Bank Board's move to limit direct investments and the effect of nonbank activities on the safety of the financial system is reviewed. S&Ls are compared with over 20 financial service industries to investigate the risk reduction potential of financial activities. The emphasis of the paper is to identify which activities are best suited for "overall risk reduction purposes." The authors conclude that real estate and commercial banking offered the best diversification potential for S&Ls. They suggest that "vertical integration into these areas could prove . . . beneficial . . . ." Woolridge and Jaffee state that "diversification into financial services would have provided relatively little risk reduction" for S&Ls "in recent years."

THRIFT INDUSTRY

1980-1984

140. Benston, George J., ed. **Financial Services: The Changing Institutions and Government Policy.** Englewood Cliffs, NJ: Prentice-Hall, Inc., 1983. 285 p. index. American Assembly, Columbia University, April 7-10, 1983.

This title is a collection of background papers presented at The American Assembly, Columbia University, from April 7-10, 1983. Recommendations on public policy issues were made by the Assembly participants. Included is an extensive bibliography. Among the authors whose papers are included are Thomas Huertas, Paul Horvitz, George Kaufman, and Edward Kane. The topics covered include the regulation of financial institutions and the role of government in the thrift crisis.

141. Carron, Andrew S. **The Rescue of the Thrift Industry.** Washington, D.C.: The Brookings Institution, 1983. 31 p.

Mr. Carron's early papers are often quoted. He has been credited with being the first to document the net worth devastation by the high rates of 1979-1980. This paper updates Mr. Carron's paper, *The Plight of the Thrift Institutions*, analyzes the legislative changes, and assesses the industry's prospects. From January 1981-November 1982 aggregated thrift data reflected deposit outflows each month. In July 1982 the Federal Reserve Board began a monetary policy to reduce interest rates; consequently, long term deposits increased. The money market deposit account was introduced in December 1982 and was very popular.

These factors reversed the deposit outflow. The author explains factors which impacted operating results negatively, such as depletion of tax refunds. He notes that the runoff experienced in 1981-1982 was called the "quiet run." The Garn-St Germain Act was passed in 1982. The regulatory merger policy is discussed, with an explanation of the "phoenix plan" given. Mr. Carron revised his forecasting model from the earlier study for this paper. He projects difficulties for several years, with a continued high rate of mergers. His prediction includes substantial consolidation of the banking industry.

142. Cassidy, Henry J. "The Role of the Savings and Loan Associations in the 1980s." In **The Savings and Loan Industry in the 1980s**, pp. 1-9. Research Working Paper No. 100. Washington, D.C.: Federal Home Loan Bank Board, December 1980. [43] p.

In a speech presented at the Third Annual Banking Conference on September 26, 1980, Mr. Cassidy's remarks pertain to the future of the industry. He views deregulation as the dominating force for the decade, with emphasis on matching maturity structures, and foresees a diversified S&L industry.

143. Gart, Alan. **The Insider's Guide to the Financial Services Revolution**. New York: McGraw-Hill Book Co., 1984. 198 p. index.

The book's focus is on all financial services, the changes in recent years, and future direction. Thrifts are included in the general discussion related to financial industry changes and future. A section is also devoted to a discussion of thrifts. The thrift problems of 1981-1982 are reviewed. A list of the largest casualties and mergers along with commentaries is included. The author reviews suggested problem solutions and industry expert forecasts.

144. Gravette, Ellis T., Jr. "The Future of the Thrift Industry". In **A Survey of Current Developments in the Thrift Industry**, pp. 9-20. Commercial Law and Practice Course Handbook Series No. 233. [New York]: Practising Law Institute, 1980. 456 p.

The effect of inflation on the industry and the economy is discussed in the beginning of this paper. The author calls on the government to take certain steps to fight the "inflationary psychology," including methods to curtail the deficit and increase personal savings. He then examines the role of thrifts in responding to disintermediation. He urges Congress to allow thrifts to be more competitive in paying rates. Among the solutions he suggests are to allow thrifts to compete on equal footing, and to restructure investment portfolios.

145. Mayer, Martin. **The Money Bazaars: Understanding the Banking Revolution Around Us.** New York: New American Library, 1984. 376 p. index.

Mr. Mayer reviews the evolution of the financial industry in the United States, and speculates on the future of banking. His book contains several references to savings institutions and presents many interesting facts and quotes. A discussion of interest rate risk notes that "More than a third of the nation's S&Ls went under in the Great Depression." The author states that the resultant "complex of federal housing and housing-finance institutions was the most successful and efficient venture of the New Deal." In the early 1960s California thrifts developed new CDs paying higher rates than passbook savings. These became so popular that it was necessary for the FHLBB to rescue the aggressive California thrifts. "Congress thereupon extended government control over interest rates to the savings associations." However, S&Ls were allowed to pay a higher interest on savings than banks. Longer term CDs were developed. The story of the development of money market funds is also told. In 1978 the FHLB-San Francisco authorized thrifts in its area to offer Variable Rate Mortgages. Proposals for various other types of mortgages soon developed, i.e. graduated payments mortgage, Canadian rollovers, shared appreciation mortgages, and the growing equity mortgage. The purchase of S&L charters by "newcomers," such as Household Finance and Sears, is also discussed. "The first depository institution to touch both shores was . . . Nationwide Savings, with offices in California, New York, and Florida, wholly owned, . . . by National Steel." The story of S&Ls is only a part of the overall thesis of this book. It is written in an absorbing, easy to read manner.

146. Meltzer, Allan H. "The Thrift Industry in the Reagan Era." In **Managing Interest Rate Risk in the Thrift Industry,** pp. 5-13. San Francisco, CA: Federal Home Loan Bank of San Francisco, [1982]. 248 p. Proceedings of the Seventh Annual Conference, December 10-11, 1981.

The problems of the thrift industry are examined in this paper. The special problems of inflation and rising interest rates are reviewed. Mr. Meltzer examines the advantages and disadvantages of adjustable mortgage loans and duration matching. He presents solutions to the problems. He comments, "When thrifts are . . . willing to compete in the consumer finance industry, they will have a better future . . . ."

147. Pratt, Richard T. "Perspective of the Chairman." In **Strategic Planning for Economic and Technological Change in the Financial Services Industry,** pp. 41-46. San Francisco, CA: Federal Home Loan Bank of San Francisco,

1983. 179 p. Proceedings of the Eighth Annual Conference, December 9-10, 1982.

Mr. Pratt discusses the Depository Institutions Deregulation Committee (DIDC), and the decisions reached by the Committee. As a committee member he describes from a personal viewpoint decisions reached regarding authorizing brokerage agreements, money market deposit accounts, super NOW accounts, selling treasury debt, and deregulating savings accounts. He warns that the next ten years will be critical for the industry. He discusses regulatory reform and the recommendation to merge the two deposit insurance agencies. Mr. Pratt concludes by saying, "I think the next 12 months will perhaps provide the greatest movement in the funds flows and realignment in financial markets that has ever occurred in this country."

148. Rosen, Kenneth T. "The Transition Problem for the Savings and Loan Industry." In **Savings and Loan Asset Management Under Deregulation**, pp. 111-114. San Francisco: Federal Home Loan Bank of San Francisco, [1981]. 377 p. Proceedings of the Sixth Annual Conference held December 8-9, 1980.

Mr. Rosen comments on the papers presented by Edward Kane and Edward Ettin at this conference. Mr. Rosen believes the tone of both papers to be too optimistic. He sees a potential housing finance crisis which "may turn the transition from a regulated to a deregulated financial structure into a catastrophe." He calls for prompt regulatory action to avoid this scenario. He views the transition crisis as being caused by volatile financial market conditions, piecemeal deregulation, inflation, and a political attack on housing and housing finance. Mr. Rosen calls for thrifts to be given the authority to pay market rates on all liabilities, tax incentives for savings, tax-exempt savings account for first-time homebuyers, alternative mortgage instruments, enforcement of due-on-sale clause, and flexibility for S&Ls to expand their non-mortgage loan portfolio.

149. Santomero, Anthony M. "Risk and Capital in Financial Institutions." In **New Sources of Capital for the Savings and Loan Industry**, pp. 35-57. San Francisco: Federal Home Loan Bank of San Francisco, [1980]. 263 p. Proceedings of the Fifth Annual Conference held December 6-7, 1979.

The opening remarks made at the end of 1979 were an explanation regarding the pressures on financial institutions in the decade: "The oil embargo and the deepest recession since the war had led to two billion-dollar bank failures, the largest disintermediation to date, and significant financial stress." The paper reviews the use of regulations to restrict risk through capital requirements. The author argues that it is necessary to control both capital and portfolio structure to regulate risk. The literature on the topic is reviewed and the social cost-benefit analysis are summarized. A model is presented. The paper concludes that concern for the mortgage market has justified regulations to restrict S&L failures. The author then asks the question, "Is this concern well founded and, if so, is it so very different from our concern about the automobile industry?" References are included.

150. **Sources of Capital for Thrifts.** [Washington, D.C.]: Federal Savings and Loan Advisory Council, Capital Adequacy Subcommittee, December 1984. 32 p. [12] p.

An in-depth study of the capital position of the savings industry was conducted. The committee found that industry capital is inadequate, and that without goodwill and appraised equity capital, it is "totally inadequate". The committee makes recommendations and urges the Bank Board to implement them. They recommend six methods of raising capital, elimination of merger impediments, methods of capital maintenance, and specific regulatory actions. They recommend elimination of RAP accounting. Capital adequacy is reviewed in detail; conversion and changes in control are examined. A lengthy assessment of other sources of capital and the need to strengthen capital requirements is included. References are given along with the presentation of tables and charts.

151. Stilwell, Joe. **The Savings & Loan Industry: Averting Collapse.** Policy Analysis. Washington, D.C.: Cato Institute, February 15, 1982. 17 p.

"Accounting procedures have created a misleading facade," the author states. He explains that the industry's net worth appears to be positive, but when studied in depth it actually has a negative net worth "in excess of $70 billion." The author examines the role of various influences on the industry, and reviews possible solutions.

152. Woerheide, Walt. **Economies of Scale in the SLA Industry: The Historical Record.** Research Working Paper No. 92. Washington, D.C.: Federal Home Loan Bank Board, February 1980. 18 p.

The imposition of interest rate ceilings in 1966 has been suggested as the cause for the shift in trends related to operating expenses. From 1952-1967 the ratio of operating expenses to total assets declined; they have risen since that time. With a shift to nonprice competition, the number of branches established have grown significantly. If interest rate ceilings are removed, the shift back to price competition may also result in a decline in operating expenses. Charts reflect operating expenses for the industry from 1950-1978.

153. Woerheide, Walter J. **The Savings and Loan Industry: Current Problems and Possible Solutions.** Westport, CT: Quorum Books, 1984. 216 p. index.

A former FHLBB economist, Mr. Woerheide, states that the purpose of this book is to examine how the industry arrived in its situation, what is being done to save the industry, and the possible consequences of these actions. The history of the System from 1932 to the 1980s, and legislation affecting the industry is reviewed. Factors influencing the profitability of S&Ls is explored in detail. Chapters are devoted to interest rate risk exposure, alternative mortgage instruments, financial futures and forward commitments, consumer lending, the elimination of interest rate ceilings, NOW accounts, and mergers and conversions. The focus of these discussions is the effects on the asset and liability sides of the balance sheet. This is a detailed review of the major developments affecting the industry from the viewpoint of the early 1980s. An extensive bibliography is included.

1985-1986

154. Balderston, Frederick E. **Thrifts in Crisis: Structural Transformation of the Savings and Loan Industry.** Cambridge, MA: Ballinger Publishing, 1985. 191 p. index.

The author has served as a regulator and on advisory panels for the FHLBB. The industry structure and its transformation are studied in detail, beginning with a history of public policy and regulation. Chapters include the discount in S&L mortgage portfolios, analysis of mergers and viability of firms, new institution entry, and the future of S&Ls. Extensive tables are included and references are provided at the end of the chapters.

155. Barth, James R., et al. **Insolvency and Risk-Taking in the Thrift Industry: Implications for the Future.** n.p., July 8, 1985. 38 p. Presented at the Annual Conference of the Western Economic Association, June 30 - July 4, 1985.

The presentation examines the historical perspective of the thrift industry, discussing risk-taking behavior of S&Ls and the FHLBB policies related to risk-taking. Recommendations are presented for dealing with the large number of insolvent institutions.

156. Benston, George J. and George G. Kaufman. "Risks and Failures in Banking: Overview, History, and Evaluation." In **Deregulating Financial Services: Public Policy in Flux**, pp. 49-77. Edited by George G. Kaufman

and Roger C. Kormendi. Cambridge, MA: Ballinger Publishing Co., 1986. 223 p.

The causes and consequences of bank runs and failures are reviewed. The adverse affects of interest rate risk on thrifts are described, noting that thrifts were able to hold rate sensitive portfolios because of deposit insurance. References given.

157. Clarke, Robert L. "The Supervisory Dilemma." In **Thrift Financial Performance and Capital Adequacy**, pp. 5-10. San Francisco, CA: Federal Home Loan Bank of San Francisco, 1987. 187 p. Proceedings of the Twelfth Annual Conference, December 11-12, 1986.

Congress wanted a healthy housing system, and viewed it as a necessity of life. Savings institutions were the means to finance that necessity. In the 1930s Congress appropriated large sums to be used to encourage the development of savings institutions. This specialization led to insolvencies in the 1980s because institutions were locked into fixed rate lending. Mr. Clarke states that banks and thrifts must be allowed to meet market demands for financial services. But the insured deposit-taking functions must be protected. He discusses FSLIC recapitalization, and urges support for it from the industry. Mr. Clarke cautions that pressure to merge FSLIC and FDIC will develop if the recap bill is not passed. He also suggests that it is difficult to continue to justify a separate industry to serve housing finance.

158. Crockett, John, Clifford Fry, and Paul Horvitz. **Equity Participation in Real Estate by Savings and Loans: Implications for Profitability and Risk.** Invited Research Working Paper No. 52. Washington, D.C.: Federal Home Loan Bank Board, May 1985. 19 p.

Opportunities and risks of equity participations are reviewed in this paper. Texas thrift experience is used for much of the paper because state-chartered institutions enjoyed a variety of real estate powers as far back as 1967. The structure of agreements is examined, as well as the risks involved, and the profitability implications. The authors state that the survey results show that "equity participations . . . have been profitable for S&L's." However, they do question the degree of risk involved and explore the facets of this question. The paper concludes by stating, "real estate equity participation per se will not produce the kinds of beneficial results for financial institutions that proponents envision."

159. Ely, Bert. **Confronting the Saving and Loan Industry Crisis.** Issue Bulletin No. 126. Washington, D.C.: The Heritage Foundation, August 13, 1986. 12 p.

Mr. Ely reviews the Bush "Recap Plan" of 1986. He also presents a plan encouraging the merger of banks and thrifts, and calls for the liquidation of FSLIC.

160. Flannery, Mark J. "Recapitalizing the Thrift Industry." In **Financial Stability of the Thrift Industry,** pp. 91-114. San Francisco: Federal Home Loan Bank of San Francisco, 1986. 230 p. Proceedings of the Eleventh Annual Conference, December 12-13, 1985.

Four alternative methods of recapitalizing the industry are discussed: internal capital growth through retained earnings; external sources of new capital; limited growth; and curtailing risks. While it is necessary for the industry to achieve adequate capitalization within a reasonable time frame to protect FSLIC, it is also necessary to impose limits on insolvent institutions to avoid unnecessary risk taking. References are included. The appendix summarizes a model for capital growth via retained earnings.

161.   Jorgensen, James. **Money Shock: Ten Ways the Financial Marketplace is Transforming Our Lives.** New York: Amacom, 1986. 224 p. index.

Two of the money shocks described by the author were when Sears began operating an S&L in California, and the fact that "passbook savings accounts are dead." The author discusses deregulation and the changes in the financial world with a slant toward the consumer. S&Ls are included in this discussion. The author says, "One of the money shocks of the 1980s is that the capital markets are on the verge of replacing savings and loans as the primary source of mortgage funds." He discusses Garn-St Germain and how it allowed thrifts to raise money cheaply. Using deposits to leverage stockholder's cash investment led to trouble for many institutions. The problems of Homestead Financial and Butterfield Savings in California are described briefly. Deposit insurance is also examined in the book. A glossary of terms is included.

162. **Outlook '86: Overview of Banking, International Finance, Securities, and Housing Policies.** Special Report, DER No. 17. Washington, D.C.: Bureau of National Affairs, Inc., January 28, 1986. [36] p.

An overview of the "groundwork for reform" began in 1985 and the prospects for FSLIC reform in 1986 is included in this report. It also discusses possible legislation and supporters of the proposed laws.

163. White, Lawrence J. "The Partial Deregulation of Banks and Other Depository Institutions." In **Regulatory Reform: What Actually Happened,** pp. 169-210. Edited by Leonard W. Weiss and Michael W. Klass. Boston: Little, Brown and Company, 1986. 316 p. index.

Economic and social regulation of depository institutions is covered by this paper. The history of regulation and an analysis of the influences on banks and thrifts is presented. Lastly, the author discusses deregulation and its consequences. He recommends risk sensitive insurance premiums, and an examination of portfolio risk. Notes and a bibliography are included.

164. Wolfson, Martin H. **Financial Crises: Understanding the Postwar U.S. Experience.** Armonk, NY: M.E. Sharpe, 1986. 228 p. index.

An overview of the S&L problems in the early 1980s is included in this book which has a broader emphasis. The author comments on thrift's strategies to surmount their problems through rapid growth, portfolio restructuring, and increasing nonmortgage loans. He also describes the role these strategies played in the "financial crises during 1984-85." Included is an overview of the run on state-insured thrifts in Ohio and Maryland in 1985. A bibliography is included.

1987-1988

165. American Bankers Association. **The FSLIC Problem: Implications for Commercial Banks.** Washington, D.C.: American Bankers Association, December 1987. 29 p.

The task force points out that S&Ls have received preferential treatment since 1966 which adversely affected banks. The paper examines alternative resolutions to FSLIC problems and discusses ABA strategy under the various scenarios.

166. American Bankers Association. **FSLIC Task Force: Report of the Chairman, William T. McConnell, to the ABA Board of Directors.** Washington, D.C.: American Bankers Association, February 12, 1988. 5 p.

The ABA Board of Directors established the task force in 1987 to represent banking's interests in the FSLIC problems. This report reviews the purpose of the task force and outlines its recommendations.

167. Brewer, Elijah. "The Current Magnitude of the Problem in the S&L Industry." In **Merging Commercial and Investment Banking**, pp. 272-284. Chicago: Federal Reserve Bank of Chicago, [1988]. 630 p. Proceedings of the 23rd Annual Conference on Bank Structure and Competition, May 6-8, 1987.

Financial figures, including profit experience for FSLIC-insured S&Ls are given in tables. The author points out that the majority of thrifts are profitable. He discusses the industry's interest rate risk exposure. Mr. Brewer states, "The problem comes not from the fact that interest rates had risen dramatically but from the fact that they rose unexpectedly."

168. Bryan, Lowell. **Perspective on the Current Thrift Crisis**. New York: McKinsey & Company, Inc., November 18, 1988. 4 p. [23] p.

Mr. Bryan prepared a report for internal use which had been discussed with "people in Washington," one of whom passed the report to the press. McKinsey received numerous requests for the report after it was mentioned in the press. This executive report was prepared to meet those requests. It includes charts containing financial information, and copies of articles appearing in newspapers and journals written by Mr. Bryan. He calls for insolvent institutions to be immediately liquidated, and advocates not selling properties in a depressed market.

169. Brown, Richard A. and Joseph A. McKenzie. **Deregulation and Portfolio Returns: The Case of Thrifts**. Research Working Paper No. 126. Washington, D.C.: Federal Home Loan Bank Board, February 12, 1987. 46 p.

The portfolio contribution of nontraditional assets are examined in this paper. The assets are multifamily mortgages, nonresidential mortgages, consumer loans, commercial loans, land acquisition and development loans, service corporation investment, and direct real estate investment. The authors state that the results show that these assets do not consistently outperform 1-4 family mortgage loans, and have a higher variance in their return than 1-4 family loans. They assert that their results "fail to corroborate the claim that nontraditional assets . . . have high yields or strong diversification benefits." References are given.

170. Ferguson, William C. **State of the Thrift Industry**. Irving, TX: Ferguson & Co., 1988. 92 p. Garn Institute of Finance, Key Largo, Florida, November 14, 1988.

These conference proceedings consist of 92 pages of tables related to the thrift industry. The first series of charts present selected financial information on a state-by-state basis. Consolidated financial information for 1985 - 6/30/88 follows. The next three sections are broken into the "haves," the "have nots," and Texas institutions. Information on GAAP solvent FSLIC thrifts is presented in a state summary, consolidated financial statements, and forecasts. The same information is presented for insolvent thrifts with additional breakdowns. An additional chart covers Southwest Plan thrifts.

171. Gatti, James F. and Ronald W. Spahr. **Discounting Negative Cash Flows and the FSLIC Case-Resolution Process.** Research Paper No. 146. Washington, D.C.: Federal Home Loan Bank Board, September 1988. 33 p.

The paper examines the problem of estimating risk-adjusted discount rates for negative cash flows when valuing FSLIC obligations. The conclusion reached by this study is that ". . . negative cash flows should be discounted as any other . . . ." The authors state that applying this analysis to the valuing of FSLIC obligations leads to the selection of the same discount rate by FSLIC and the acquirer. References are included.

172. Hirschhorn, Eric. **Interest Rates on Thrift Certificates of Deposit.** Washington, D.C.: Federal Home Loan Bank Board, December 1988. [5] p.

Beginning in January 1987, FSLIC insured thrifts reported offer rates for a variety of deposit accounts. Fourteen different CDs are included. Mr. Hirschhorn summarizes the developments in the offer rates and discusses the Texas premium. Charts illustrate the offerings. The author states, "The relationship between the financial condition of offering institutions and the rates they pay is readily apparent . . . Well capitalized thrifts generally pay rates that are slightly below industry averages and insolvent institutions pay rates somewhat above industry average rates." He also notes that (at this point in time), "Only at GAAP-insolvent institutions are jumbo rates still above the yields on Treasury securities." The charts presented for Texas institutions "indicate that there has indeed been a Texas premium . . . the concentration of relatively weak thrifts in Texas drives up average rates in the state . . . regardless of condition. As a result, the Texas premium has been a real phenomenon, not just a reflection of the extent of problems in the state." The paper proceeds by explaining that the Texas premium has declined over the past seven quarters, having reached its peak in June 1987. The resolutions since the implementation of the Southwest Plan has added to the decline in rates. The author closes by noting, "statistical evidence suggests that removing high paying institutions will lead to rate reductions in the remaining elements of the industry."

173. Kaufman, George G. "Public Policy Toward Failing Institutions: The Lessons From the Thrift Industry." In **Merging Commercial and Investment Banking**, pp. 267-271. Chicago: Federal Reserve Bank of Chicago, [1988]. 630 p. Proceedings of the 23rd Annual Conference on Bank Structure and Competition, May 6-8, 1987.

In this short essay Mr. Kaufman stresses that people need to be convinced there is an S&L crisis. He says policy makers are not urging "repairs", and the public is not calling for changes. He touches on the problems in Ohio, Maryland, Vernon S&L, First South Federal in Pine Bluff Arkansas, and Franklin SA in Kansas. He urges a change in public policy to stop further abuses.

174. National Council of Savings Institutions. **The FSLIC Crisis: Assessments and Recommendations.** Washington, D.C.: National Council of Savings Institutions, 1988. 17 p.

The report maintains that it is "the first proposal offered by a major thrift industry group to resolve the . . . FSLIC crisis." The recommendations were drafted by a task force composed of CEOs of insured financial institutions. The recommendations are: transfer all FSLIC insured institutions meeting capital standards to FDIC; insolvent institutions should remain in FSLIC for disposition; fund the bailout from Federal Home Loan Bank System retained earnings, and a loan from the Treasury; expand membership in the FHLB System to other financial institutions; and maintain the dual banking system. Financial figures are given in tables.

175. Pressman, Steven. **Behind the S&L Crisis.** Editorial Research Reports. Washington, D.C.: Congressional Quarterly, November 4, 1988. 14 p.

Mr. Pressman presents a brief overview of the crisis in this report. Covered are the questions related to the cost of the bailout, deregulation, oil problems, Ohio and Maryland crises, and possible solutions.

176. Riedy, Mark J. **New Capital, New Structure: Are They the Twin Needs of the Thrift Industry?** Opening Address, Western States' 1988 Convention, Sun Valley, Idaho, September 21, 1988. 9 p.

Mark Riedy made this presentation as president of the National Council of Savings Institutions. Mr. Riedy identifies two problems facing the industry:

GAAP net worth, and the structure of the industry and its future role in the financial services system. He calls for the thrift industry to offer solutions to its own problems. He reflects that franchise value must be preserved, and a regulatory infrastructure must be forged which will allow institutions to build value. The safety and soundness of the deposit insurance system should be restored. He criticizes the idea that healthy institutions should bear the cost of resolving the problems. He emphasizes that thrifts "should hoard jealously your remaining equity capital." The address reviews other issues the Council is studying. Mr. Riedy emphasizes that the Council supports risk-based deposit insurance. He concludes by remarking that the industry must provide "extraordinary leadership" in the coming months.

177. Rose, Peter S. **The Changing Structure of American Banking**. New York: Columbia University Press, 1987. 419 p. index.

A chapter is devoted to thrift institutions in which Mr. Rose presents an overview of changes in the S&L industry, and discusses the 1980 DIDMCA. It is noted that there were more than 6300 institutions at year-end 1960, compared with 3391 institutions at year-end 1984. The decline is attributed to economic forces which redefined the industry, leading to a significant number of mergers in the 1970s and early 1980s. During the same time span the industry was stressed by its asset base and interest costs. The author states, "The specter of hundreds of S&L failures . . . prompted . . . In 1980 the DIDMCA" being passed. He further notes that, "Not fully satisfied with the results of these innovations, Congress made a second pass at the problem in October 1982 with passage of the Garn-St Germain Depository Institutions Act." This short chapter provides a synopsis of the industry.

178. Sherman, Eugene J. **Credit Worthiness of the Consolidated Obligations of the Federal Home Loan Banks**. New York: Federal Home Loan Bank of New York, February 27, 1987. 21 p.

This paper is a summary of remarks presented to the Treasury Securities Luncheon Club. Mr. Sherman was Chief Economist at the FHLB-New York. In the introduction he states that he is reviewing the System credit worthiness because of the thrift industry problems. He also discusses the profitability of the industry and the FSLIC recapitalization bill. Charts included compare the Bank System to the four largest profitable banks. The System is larger in total assets than all but Citicorp, and has more equity capital than any of the major profitable banks. The System's return on assets are higher than three of the major banks. The point is also made that the System banks have suffered no losses over their 55-year history. In discussing the thrift industry in general Mr. Sherman points out that the Bank System has rigid collateral requirements, and that the Banks' assets are well secured. He notes that 80% of the thrift institutions in the U.S. are profitable. Several charts reflect the state of the institutions. The author discusses the need for a FSLIC recapitalization bill.

179. **U.S. League of Savings Institutions Report of the Task Force on FSLIC Issues.** [Washington, D.C.]: U.S. League of Savings Institutions, [January 1987]. 54 p.

The report points out that earlier funding plans for FSLIC were based on limited knowledge of the funding requirements. Based on subsequent information regarding the severity of the problem, new proposals are presented. The thesis is that regional economic problems are creating unforeseen difficulties, and that programs are needed to help well-managed institutions survive these problems. Additionally, a flexible program to meet the needs of deposit insurance is offered. The result suggested is a "Savings Institutions Self-Help Plan". The League calls for the FHLBB to adopt a forebearance policy for well managed institutions located in economic disaster areas. Secondly, they suggest funding FSLIC with a blending of the 1986 League "Pay-As-You-Go" Plan and the Treasury/Bank Board Recapitalization Plan.

180. Wall, M. Danny. "Toward a Healthy, Competitive Thrift Industry." In **Expanded Competitive Markets and the Thrift Industry**, pp. 5-14. San Francisco: Federal Home Loan Bank of San Francisco, [1988]. 227 p. Proceedings of the Thirteenth Annual Conference held December 10-11, 1987.

Mr. Wall was sworn in as chairman of the FHLBB on July 1, 1987. Mr. Wall first points out that the S&L industry restructuring is not unlike the restructuring occurring in many industries in the U.S. and internationally. He emphasizes that the FSLIC recapitalization of 1986-1987 was similar to the Credit Union Share Insurance Fund recapitalization shortly after the passage of the Garn-St Germain bill. The challenges to the FDIC fund are mentioned. A review is given of the changes in the examination responsibilities at the FHLBB and FHLB System, and other changes under consideration are outlined. Comments are made on the MCP program and FSLIC case resolutions.

1989

181. Balderston, Frederick E. **The S&L Bailout: A Policy Review.** Berkeley, CA: Institute of Business and Economic Research, University of California, 1989. 23 p.

Mr. Balderston reviews the 1989 bailout from different points focusing on the various methods of financing the bailout. He also discusses regulatory and monitoring structure.

182. Benston, George J. and Michael F. Koehn. **Capital Dissipation, Deregulation, and the Insolvency of Thrifts.** Rolling Hill Estate, CA: Analysis Group, Inc., 1989. 17 p.

The paper focuses on three hypotheses to explain the crisis: specialization and forbearance, mispriced deposit insurance and interest rate deregulation, and asset deregulation. Legislation and regulation relative to the three possibilities is discussed. The hypotheses are "tested" and conclusions are reached using data from California institutions. A bibliography is included.

183. Bisenius, Donald J. **Dividend Payments by Thrifts.** Special Report. Washington, D.C.: Federal Home Loan Bank Board, September 1989. 6 p.

As of December 1988 over 40% of FSLIC-insured thrifts were stockholder owned; only 23% paid dividends in the fourth quarter 1988. The average number of institutions paying dividends varied from 13% in 1984 to 23% in 1988. The payout ratio is divergent with the bulk paying less than 40% of net income, but several paying out all of their income. The dividend behavior at thrifts which converted during the early 1980s reflects an increase in payments. OTS is proposing consolidation and revision of rules governing dividend payments. Charts illustrate the dividend information.

184. Caso, Edward S., Jr., Robert G. Hottensen, Jr., and Jennifer A. Wilson. **S&L Bill's Impact on Federal Home Loan Banks/Thrifts.** n.p.: Goldman Sachs, June 21, 1989. 30 p.

The role of the Federal Home Loan Bank System in the resolution process and its ultimate effect on the thrift industry is examined. Projections on the decrease in earnings available to pay dividends are made. Tables present earnings information and names institutions in various categories with impact projections.

185. **Combined Financial Statements: SAIF-Insured Associations.** Washington, D.C.: Office of Thrift Supervision, 1989. 88 p.

Balance sheet, income, and expense information is presented for thrift institutions on an aggregated basis. The information is available for the U.S., district, and by state. Previous editions of this title were published by the FHLBB. **Combined Financial Statements, FSLIC-Insured Institutions** was published from 1983-1988. The title of the publication for the years 1970-1982 was **Combined Financial Statements, FSLIC-Insured Savings and Loan Associations.**

186. Eichler, Ned. **The Thrift Debacle.** Berkeley, CA: University of California Press, 1989. 163 p.

The history of S&Ls is traced in this title showing how deregulation led to disaster. Regulations of the 1930s and 1980s are compared and similarities are noted. Mr. Eichler states that the "New Dealers" were desperate to prop up the collapsing mortgage market and to promote home construction in 1929. Therefore, they "decided to insure savings and loan deposits." The 1955 decline in industry profits was the beginning of the push for deregulation. A lengthy assessment of deregulation is presented. The text provides insight into events and weaves into the S&L story the rapid growth of GNP, the economy and the housing market, interest rates, real estate prices, and inflation rates. Included is a review of housing production, sales, and finance. The author reflects that in 1970 government subsidies for housing constituted 29.2% of total housing production. He states that the "Public opted to have federal government foster home ownership." Mr. Eichler provides an assessment of what should have been done for the industry suggesting that the Bank Board should have pushed harder for authority to make variable rate loans. He also reviews the terms of FHLBB chairmen Janis, Pratt, Gray, and Wall. A selective bibliography appears at the end of the text.

187. Gart, Alan. **An Analysis of the New Financial Institutions: Changing Technologies, Financial Structures, Distribution Systems, and Deregulation.** New York: Quorum Books, 1989. 376 p. index.

With the blurring of lines between services provided by banks, insurance companies, and investment banking firms, the financial services industry will consolidate into three power bases. Mr. Gart explores the changes in the various industry players, and discusses the future as he sees it. One section of this book is devoted to S&Ls. A brief history is given along with a more detailed review of the events of the late 1980s. Comparisons are made between state and federal chartered institutions, and stock and mutuals. A chart lists the number and assets of S&Ls by charter type and year. Specific discussions are included on disintermediation and mismatched maturities, competition and structure, hedging, ARMs, swaps, secondary market activities, and brokered deposits. These discussions provide an overview of the S&L business, its problems, and earning potential.

188. Greider, William. **The Trouble With Money.** The Larger Agenda Series. Knoxville, TN: Whittle Direct Books, 1989. 94 p.

The author reviews economic issues and argues that reregulation is inevitable. Among the issues discussed are banks and the "too big to fail" doctrine, high interest rates, and the S&L crisis. He discusses specific institutions and individuals.

189. Howe, Robert. **Restructuring the Savings and Loan Industry: Bibliography-in-Brief, 1986-1989.** CRS Report for Congress 89-162L. Washington, D.C.: Congressional Research Service, Library of Congress, February 1989. 9 p.

Divided into three parts the bibliography focuses on background materials related to the industry, issues of deposit insurance, and policy issues.

190. Kane, Edward J. **The S & L Insurance Mess: How Did It Happen?** Washington, D.C.: The Urban Institute Press, 1989. 181 p.

The role capital played in aggressive growth strategies undertaken by S&L management is explained by the author. He discusses the role of PACs in the industry, and the "political roots" of forbearance. A table listing the top beneficiaries from S&L PAC donations is included. Critical mistakes in FSLIC policy are identified. Mr. Kane also discusses why it was not in the best interest of politicians or regulators to close insolvent thrifts early. The last chapter of the book is a detailed discussion of suggestions for reform. References are included at the end of the chapters.

191. Kaufman, George G. "Framework for the Future: Resurrecting and Legitimizing the Thrift Industry." In **The Future of the Thrift Industry,** pp. 191-207. San Francisco: Federal Home Loan Bank of San Francisco, 1989. 253 p. Proceedings of the Fourteenth Annual Conference, December 8-9, 1988.

Various methods of restructuring the banking system are mentioned. Presented in detail is the proposal in two parts by George Benston and Mr. Kaufman. First, net worth requirements are increased so institutions have their own funds at risk.   Secondly, a procedure for insurance agency intervention on a mandatory basis is instituted. Predetermined capital/asset ratio tranches are established. Tables illustrate the reorganization rules and applicable tranches. While encouraging adoption of this proposal the author points out that "current policies have succeeded primarily in redigging the hole to the level it was in 1981, after it was temporarily filled by a fall in interest rates." Restructuring the industry will require timely insolvency intervention and higher capital requirements. The panelists for discussion of this presentation are William Isaac, Richard Syron, and Lawrence White.

192. Kaufman, George G. **The Savings and Loan Rescue of 1989: Causes and Perspective.** Working Paper Series: Issues in Financial Regulation 89-23. Chicago: Federal Reserve Bank of Chicago, November 1989. 20 p.

The author points out that the government financial assistance for the S&L crisis dwarfs the previous bailouts to New York City and Chrysler ". . . by a factor of some 50 and 80 respectively." The stringent regulation of thrifts since 1933 forced institutions to assume interest rate and capital risk. Building on this basic fact Mr. Kaufman reviews the major factors contributing to the industry demise. He then recaps the primary components of FIRREA. The future of the industry is explored. References are included. This paper is also included in **Restructuring the American Financial System,** edited by George G. Kaufman.

193. **Management Agreement Among the Federal Home Loan Bank Board, the Federal Savings and Loan Insurance Corporation, and the Federal Deposit Insurance Corporation.** Washington, D.C.: Federal Home Loan Bank Board, February 7, 1989. 30 p.

In the management agreement the FHLBB "consents to the engagement by the FSLIC of the FDIC to assist the FSLIC in the discharge of its duties as Receiver." The agreement spells out budget provisions, personnel issues, cooperation between the agencies, and indemnifies the FDIC.

194. Miller, Richard B. **American Banking in Crisis: Views from Leading Financial Services CEOS.** Homewood, IL: Dow Jones-Irwin, 1989. 178 p. index.

Mr. Miller interviewed twenty CEOs regarding what they felt the industry problems or issues are and the possible solutions. Woven into the discussions are quotes from the CEOs related to the topic. Among the subjects discussed are bank management, regulation, economic crises, lending, and competition. Thrifts are mentioned in various sections with one lengthy discussion of the industry problems. The overwhelming view of the thrift crisis seems to be that it has hurt the entire financial industry, and has adversely impacted the chances of banks obtaining additional powers. The CEOs reviewed are very critical of thrifts indicating a feeling that their problems relate to poor management. Many feel there is no place for thrifts in the financial industry. They also expressed concern over the effect the problem is having on interest margins for all financial institutions. The executives gave their views on various proposals related to deposit insurance reform.

195. Oros, John J. "Strategies for Capital Adequacy." In **Strategies for the Nineties**, pp. 149-163. San Francisco: Federal Home Loan Bank of San Francisco, [1990]. 197 p. Proceedings of the Fifteenth Annual Conference held December 14-15, 1989.

Mr. Oros begins his presentation by reviewing financial figures for the thrift industry. He considers the industry assets and the redeployment necessary to deal with the crisis. He states, "If all current insolvent institutions were merged with healthy institutions rather than liquidated, FSLIC-insolvent thrifts would require additional capital nearly equal to the current capitalization of the entire industry." Using TB 36 (capital requirements) he discusses RTC institutions, presenting charts which illustrate capitalization, net worth, asset composition, and real estate owned (REO). The author continues by comparing the banking and thrift industries. He points out that bank assets are diversified; they are advantaged with non-interest-bearing deposits and have access to unsecured borrowing markets. Lastly, he remarks on the consolidation of financial institutions in other countries, and suggests that the U.S. will move in a similar direction. The panel discussions on this topic were presented by Gerald Barrone and Robert Barnes.

196. Spellman, Lewis J. and Douglas O. Cook. "Reducing Default Premia on Insured Deposits: The Policy Alternatives." In **The Future of the Thrift Industry**, pp. 169-185. San Francisco: Federal Home Loan Bank of San Francisco, 1989. 253 p. Proceedings of the Fourteenth Annual Conference, December 8-9, 1988.

FSLIC losses have resulted in the careful evaluation of firm-specific risk in pricing deposit liabilities. Investors are looking at individual institution's strength rather than depending on deposit insurance. The motivation for the "Southwest Plan" was to reduce the high cost of funds influenced by the Texas premium. The purpose of this paper is to establish if the default risk premia are the result of firm risk variables or if they are influenced by a loss of confidence in FSLIC. Three policy alternatives and their effect on the premia are investigated: infusion of capital, the upgrade of the deposit guarantee, and an increase in the FSLIC premium. Institutions in the Eleventh District were used for the analysis. References are given.

197. Wall, M. Danny. "The Tasks Ahead." In **The Future of the Thrift Industry**, pp. 231-237. San Francisco: Federal Home Loan Bank of San Francisco, 1989. 253 p. Proceedings of the Fourteenth Annual Conference, December 8-9, 1988.

Mr. Wall discusses the state of the industry by presenting financial numbers for the year. He discusses in detail the "size of the problem" and possible resolution methods. He also presents various proposals to prevent recurrence of the situation. He calls for broader membership in the FHLB System. Deposit insurance premiums are discussed. In 1934 actuaries recommended premiums of 32 basis points as compared with the 25 basis points in effect. Congress did not accept the recommendation, and actually lowered the premiums which indicated that the government would be the ultimate guarantor. Mr. Wall states, "Here we are, 54 years later, experiencing what can be identified as a 100-year flood. Now it is time to deal with the promise made in 1935 to service all . . . categories of losses." The Chairman of the Bank Board points out that Congress is committed to the industry. He closes by stating that 80% of S&Ls are profitable.

198. Wells, F. Jean. **The FSLIC Issue: A Status Report.** CRS Report for Congress 89-77E. Washington, D.C.: Congressional Research Service, Library of Congress, February 2, 1989. 4 p.

This report is very general in nature. It is intended as a very brief overview of the thrift industry problem and the legislative outlook based on fact finding hearings.

199. Wells, F. Jean. **FSLIC Policy Options.** CRS Report for Congress 89-56E. Washington, D.C.: Congressional Research Service, Library of Congress, January 26, 1989. 6 p.

Ms. Wells reviews the four policy proposals in place at the time of publication to deal with the insolvent insurance fund.

200. Woodward, G. Thomas. **FSLIC, the Budget, and the Economy.** CRS Report for Congress 89-17E. Washington, D.C.: Congressional Research Service, Library of Congress, January 12, 1989. 8 p.

The effect on the federal deficit of FSLIC recapitalization is reviewed in this paper. It also examines the possible effects on interest rates and inflation.

1990

201. Brown, Richard A., Joseph A. McKenzie, and Rebel A. Cole. **Going Beyond Traditional Mortgages: The Portfolio Performance of Thrifts.** Financial Industry Studies Working Paper No. 1-90. Dallas: Federal Reserve Bank of Dallas, February 1990. 25 p.

An evaluation of investment restrictions re-imposed on thrifts by FIRREA is the purpose of this paper. Cost accounting methodology is used to estimate average returns on alternative portfolio investments of FSLIC-insured institutions for the year ending 6-30-88. Separate analyses are conducted by net worth for three groups of S&Ls. The results show that consumer loans and multifamily mortgages were comparable to home mortgages; non-traditional areas provided significantly lower returns especially for insolvent thrifts. The authors state that these findings "are far more pronounced at tangible-insolvent institutions lending support [to] the hypothesis that insolvent thrifts used nontraditional investments as a means to exploit a faulty deposit insurance system." The authors argue for reform of the deposit insurance system and prompt closure of insolvent institutions. They further assert that investment restrictions expose healthy thrifts to interest-rate risk; that restrictions should apply to insolvent institutions which do not bear the cost of their risk. References are included.

202. Bryan, Lowell. **Restoring Health and Profitability to the U.S. Banking System.** [N.Y.]: McKinsey & Co., 1990. 49 p. [31] p.

This study plays a part in Mr. Bryan's later book **Bankrupt.** He discusses the reasons for the current banking system problems which are visible in the credit crunch. He describes the reforms which are needed for a sound banking industry. S&Ls and BIF are mentioned only to emphasize the need to restructure insolvent institutions as early as possible.

203. Ferguson, William C. **State of the Thrift Industry 1989-1990.** Irving, TX: Ferguson & Co., [1990]. 39 p.

Mr. Ferguson reviews the state of the industry. He gives an overview of private sector thrifts (those not under RTC control), noting that at the end of 1989 there were 1,992 institutions not under RTC control with tangible capital equivalent to more than 3% of tangible assets. He states that barring severe economic declines most of these institutions should prosper. A group of 357 institutions with tangible assets in the 0%-3% range should find solutions to operating difficulties and be able to prosper. He also discusses three additional groups, defined as "potential failures," "potential survivors," and "terminally ill." He calls for more resources and aggressive programs to assist the "potential survivors." Mr. Ferguson continues by offering a "1990 Outlook for the Industry." He states that "The fundamental determinant of the prospective health and vitality of the thrift industry is not economic, it is political." He discusses the priorities for the industry in 1990: regulatory policy reform, appointments of key officials, effective case resolution programs, assistance to potential survivors, and restoring the value of the thrift charter. He concludes by stating that a substantial thrift industry can survive, and a number of undercapitalized thrifts can achieve market place solutions if there are not "hidden time bombs" in the industry. Twenty-five pages of charts are included in the paper. The charts present data on thrifts not under RTC control on a state-by-state basis, giving capital, and historical figures. Information is also presented for thrifts under RTC control.

204. Harris, Jack C. **The Savings and Loan Crisis**. College Station, TX: Texas A&M University, 1990. 14 p.

Thrift profitability problems caused by economic turbulence during the 1980s are reviewed. The author states, "The savings and loan crisis is the story of how a system designed for stability unraveled when faced with extraordinary turbulence." Mr. Harris writes that additional controls are not the remedy for the situation because reform of flawed systems and removal of problem regulations are needed. The future of the industry with an emphasis on the regulatory system is also discussed.

205. Hendershott, Patric H. and James D. Shilling. **The Continued Interest Rate Vulnerability of Thrifts**. NBER Working Paper Series No. 3415. Cambridge, MA: National Bureau of Economic Research, August 1990. 36 p.

The author states that thrifts were still using 40% of their short-term deposits to fund long term mortgage loans in early 1989. He asserts that thrifts could experience a $100-$130 billion cash flow loss if the rate cycle of 1977-1986 were to be repeated. Mr. Hendershott presents an analysis of thrift interest-rate sensitivity. The author's conclusion is that "Taxpayers will continue to be at substantial risk until the thrift industry is either recapitalized or liquidated." References precede notes and tables which conclude the paper.

206. Kaufman, George G. "The Savings and Loan Rescue of 1989: Causes and Perspectives." In **Restructuring the American Financial System**, pp. 57-69. Edited by George G. Kaufman. Boston: Kluwer Academic Publishers, 1990. 180 p. index.

Mr. Kaufman begins by pointing out that the bailout was not of thrift owners or managers; they lost their investments or jobs. The bailout was of S&L depositors who received the full amount of their deposits. The author states, "The bailout represents a redistribution from taxpayers who did not have insured deposits at insolvent associations to taxpayers . . . who did . . . ." The causes of the crisis are capsulized. Among those listed are: stringent regulation resulting in interest rate risk and credit risk; increasing the deposit insurance ceiling; liberalizing deposit rates; brokered deposits; understaffing of the FHLB

System regulatory staff; political contributions; and lack of timely Congressional response. Mr. Kaufman lists the important aspects of FIRREA. References are given. This paper is essentially the same as the one published by the Federal Reserve Bank of Chicago by the same title.

207. Langston, E.A. **Understanding the S&L Crisis.** Washington, D.C.: Squeaky Wheel Press, 1990. 27 p. illus.

Using black and white illustrations and simple terminology, the crisis and its history is explained. Included are "pre-outraged" postcards for ease in communicating with Congressional representatives.

208. **The 1989 Gallup Study on the Savings and Loan Crisis: Summary Report and Cross Tabular Analysis.** Study No. 89119. Princeton, NJ: The Gallup Organization, Inc., June 1990. 355 p.

During May 1989 telephone interviews were held with 1,298 financial decision-makers nationwide. S&L depositors were questioned regarding their knowledge of deposit insurance and awareness of failing institutions. Also explored were the incentives created by higher interest rates and depositors willingness to use institutions located out-of-town. They found that people's knowledge was limited related to S&L problems, about 25% of depositors were concerned with the safety of their deposits, and that location was more important to those surveyed than earning a 2% higher rate would be.

209. **The Savings & Loan Debacle.** DPS Special Report-The Savings and Loan Crisis No. 36. [Washington, D.C.: Senate Democratic Policy Committee], October 29, 1990. 28 p.

This document is especially interesting from the standpoint of the language used to describe the crisis by the publishing agency. The paper provides an overview of the situation beginning with the 1970s, breaking down the problems into "the five phases of the S&L quandary." The phases are: disintermediation; mismatched assets and liabilities; deregulation; attempts to solve asset quality problems; and FIRREA. The paper notes that "the mess" could have been cleaned up a decade ago at a much lower cost. Each of the phases is described in detail presenting information on reform proposals and the reaction by the administration and the political parties. The author states that the early solutions to the thrift problems "were the foundations of later problems." It is noted that in 1981, $30 billion was requested to solve the problem and this request was ignored. Also in 1981 the Democratic "regulators bill" called "for a $3 billion line of credit with the Treasury . . . Instead the Reagan Administration's push for deregulation won and the solutions to problems were delay . . . The result of a decade long attempt to avoid a taxpayer bailout . . . has left taxpayer(s) with a larger bill . . . ." The paper ends by stating that the soundness of thrifts will continue to be an issue.

210. Waldman, Michael. **Who Robbed America? A Citizen's Guide to the S&L Scandal.** New York: Random House, 1990. 249 p.

With an introduction by Ralph Nader, this book compiled by the staff of Public Citizen's Congress Watch, is a "call to action" for America's citizens. The thesis is that taxpayers are bearing the cost of the bailout due to lobbyists and political action committees (PACs) influence on Congress. Included is a history of S&Ls, with specifics on Lincoln S&L and Silverado. Congressmen, regulators, lawyers, accountants, and Southwest Plan participants are taken to task. Solutions and individual action plans are offered. Detailed appendices list congressional votes and PAC donations, as well as institution failures by state. A resource list is included.

1991-1992

211. **Aggregated Thrift Financial Reports.** Washington, D.C.: Office of Thrift Supervision, 1992. 1320 p.

Aggregated financial information for the United States, OTS regions, and by state are presented. The information is detailed, corresponding to the thrift financial reports filed by individual institutions. The line item names match the TFR. Thirty pages of aggregated data are available for each breakdown included. Prior to FIRREA quarterly aggregated information was released by the FHLBB. The information was available on a semi-annual basis prior to 1984.

212. Barth, James R. **The Great Savings and Loan Debacle.** Washington, D.C.: The AEI Press, 1991. 170 p.

Mr. Barth tells the S&L "story" so it will be understood, and to prevent similar events in the future. He points out that the industry was insolvent before deregulation. He begins by presenting S&L history from 1830 through the "turbulent 1980s". He then reviews FIRREA and continues with a discussion of deposit insurance and the need for reform. The text includes detailed tables, appendices covering industry powers, regulation, and legislation. An extensive bibliography is included.

213. Bryan, Lowell L. **Bankrupt: Restoring the Health and Profitability of Our Banking System.** N.Y.: HarperBusiness, 1991. 315 p. index.

Mr. Bryan states that our "obsolete regulation is destroying not only our banks but our economy." He writes about reforming the regulation of commercial banks. In this context he discusses the S&L debacle, its causes and consequences. He points out that the industry by 1981, "had almost no real capital left." He states that the insolvent S&Ls should have been closed at that time, and the rest converted to banks. The chapter on S&Ls discusses the political and regulatory decisions which contributed to the debacle. Mr. Bryan ends the chapter by noting that he believes a separate thrift industry is not needed; therefore, the solutions for reforming the S&L industry are the same as those for the banking industry.

214. Kane, Edward J. **The S&L Insurance Mess.** Contemporary Issues Series 41. St. Louis, MO: Center for the Study of American Business, Washington University, February 1991. 23 p.

Comparing Congress, the FHLBB and FSLIC to Mickey Mouse as sorcerer in *Fantasia*, and S&Ls to "zombies" feeding on taxpayers, Mr. Kane was the first to use these analogies. He explains his inferences in this pamphlet. He traces the interest rate increases induced by the Vietnam War as the beginning of the S&L problems. The tightening of money in 1979-1980 to reduce inflation is credited as the second stage of the problem which caused rapid interest rate increases from 1979-1982. Insolvencies increased, but officials pursued avenues to keep institutions in business. Mr. Kane explores regulatory failures, deposit insurance subsidies, S&L self-dealing, and inept management. Also discussed is the cost and need for political reform. This short pamphlet is informative, to the point, and includes a list of suggested taxpayer actions.

215. Lowy, Martin. **High Rollers: Inside the Savings and Loan Debacle.** N.Y.: Praeger, 1991. 321 p. index.

Martin Lowy states that he wants "to tell you the S&L story the way the professionals see it." He bases this story on his twenty-five years experience as a lawyer and banker. He stresses that fraud played only a small role in the crisis; the blames lies with Congress, the regulators, and "everyone who had a fixed-rate mortgage . . . or thrift CD." He reviews the regulatory structure of thrifts and accounting rules, discusses specific S&L problems and the politics involved. He ends by exploring deposit insurance reform and the future of specialized housing lenders. A bibliography is provided.

216. O'Connell, William B. **America's Money Trauma: How Washington Blunders Crippled the U.S. Financial System.** n.p.: Conversation Press, Inc., 1992. 156 p. index.

Mr. O'Connell writes from the perspective of past president of the U. S. League of Savings Institutions. A history of deregulation, focusing on the errors involved, is presented. The years reviewed cover the Carter Administration through the Reagan Administration. The author states that "American taxpayers angry about savings institution and bank failures . . . should focus their outrage on key players on the Washington scene." The book begins with the deregulation of deposit interest rates and covers the DIDC, Garn-St Germain, the 1986 Tax Reform Act, and FIRREA. The role of Paul Volcker and the Federal Reserve are explored in a chapter dealing with the interest rate scenario. A chapter devoted to the FHLBB contains sections on former chairmen Jay Janis, Richard Pratt, Edwin Gray, M. Danny Wall, and L. William Seidman. The role of these gentlemen in the crisis is reviewed. Mr. O'Connell also comments on the RTC and Charles Keating.

217. Romer, Thomas and Barry R. Weingast. "Political Foundations of the Thrift Debacle." In **The Reform of Federal Deposit Insurance: Disciplining the Government and Protecting Taxpayers**, pp. 167-202. Edited by James R. Barth and R. Dan Brumbaugh. [N.Y.]: HarperBusiness, 1992. 310 p. index.

The political aspects of the thrift debacle and the role of elected officials is the focus of this essay. The Garn-St Germain Act eased regulations and relaxed regulatory accounting. The author poses several questions: Why were thrifts allowed to "gamble for resurrection?"; Why did Congress respond so slowly?; and Why was the 1987 legislation "too little, too late?" Congress established a policy of forbearance. "Congressional behavior with respect to the thrift industry should be seen as fairly routine politics, rather than as an outrageous deviation." Various aspects of the relationship between Congress and regulatory agencies is discussed in great detail. The authors contend that interest groups make it difficult for Congress to deal with problems at an early stage. Because taxpayers do not see legislators as playing a role in the problem, they are not penalized for letting the problem grow. References are contained in the essay. This paper was also published in June 1990 by the Graduate School of Industrial Administration, Carnegie-Mellon University, Pittsburgh, PA, as GSIA Working Paper #1190-14.

218. Shoven, John B., Scott B. Smart, and Joel Waldfogel. **Real Interest Rates and the Savings and Loan Crisis: The Moral Hazard Premium.** NBER Working Paper Series No. 3754. Cambridge, MA: National Bureau of Economic Research, 1991. 29 p.

The authors examine the question of why real interest rates were significantly higher in the 1980s. They review popular explanations and present their theory.

Their theory relates high real interest rates to the savings and loan crisis, and that the yield on Treasury bills increased to allow them to remain competitive with S&L deposit yields. The additional cost to the government debt for the high yields are calculated and projected in the appendix. References are provided.

219. Southern Finance Project. **Under New Management: The S&L Crisis and the Rural South.** Charlotte, N.C.: Southern Finance Project, July 1992. 106 p.

This report reviews the S&L restructuring which has occurred and the effects on the rural South. The report states that institutions in poorer counties were more likely to be liquidated than those in affluent counties, and that by the end of 1990, two-thirds of the poor counties had no S&L branches. It is also suggested that the supply of first-tier housing credit may shrink with the demise of local thrifts. The authors present five initiatives for reforming RTC practices and restructuring deposit insurance. The report calls for institutions in conservatorships to be "given or marketed" to "community development financial institutions," or "converted into democratically-controlled 'public purpose' banks," which will be "better attuned to the nation's credit needs . . . ." The report contains thirty tables and graphs, and thirty-six pages of appendices. These reflect institutions in conservatorship, branch information by county, portfolio characteristics of thrifts with rural branches, simulation of OTS solvency rankings, data related to lending by branch, and other detailed information supporting the text. A bibliography is included.

220. Stewart, Alva W. **The Savings and Loan Crisis: A Bibliography.** Public Administration Series: Bibliography #P 3074. Monticello, IL: Vance Bibliographies, April 1991. 11 p.

Included in this bibliography are newspaper and journal articles, books, government documents, and Congressional hearings. The time period covered is 1988 - October 1990. This is a selective bibliography.

221. Taylor, Jeremy F. **The Keepers of Finance: U.S. Financial Leadership at the Crossroads.** New York: Quorum Books, 1991. 237 p. index.

The leadership needed to rebuild the U.S. financial system is the focus of this title. References to S&Ls are woven throughout the book. In discussing the S&L problem the author states, "The pre-bailout examination of S&Ls often relied on audits by outside accounting firms, the competency of which came into real question. The Federal Home Loan Bank Board was not stringent in its examination requirements." Charles Keating and Lincoln S&LA, and Tom

Spiegel at Columbia S&L (junk bond losses) are discussed. The resolution process has "proved inadequate". RTC funding is inadequate and Refcorp has had problems in marketing bonds to finance the bailout. The author describes morale and leadership problems in the bailout agencies. A selected bibliography is included.

222. White, Lawrence J. **The S&L Debacle: Public Policy Lessons for Bank and Thrift Regulation.** N.Y.: Oxford University Press, 1991. 287 p. index.

A board member of the Federal Home Loan Bank Board from 1986-1989, Mr. White writes from this perspective, as well as his background as an economist. He reviews the "debacle"--how and why it happened. He points to the thrift regulatory system, deposit insurance, deregulation, and the cleanup legislation. CEBA and FIRREA are also discussed. The last section of the book discusses reform of deposit insurance and bank and thrift regulation. Numerous tables, extensive notes, and a lengthy bibliography are included.

COMPETITIVE
EQUALITY BANKING
ACT OF 1987

223. **CEBA Guide: Questions and Answers.** Washington, D.C.: Federal
Home Loan Bank System, 1988. 97 p.

This guide was prepared by the Office of Regulatory Policy, Oversight and
Supervision. General information is provided on certain sections of the
Competitive Equality Banking Act of 1987. The book is presented in a question
and answer format. The introduction states that, "The questions answered in
this guide are those most commonly asked by examination and supervisory staff
. . . during CEBA training . . . ." The topics covered are accounting,
appraisals, debt restructuring, classification of assets, capital, QTL, applications,
and the S&L holding company act.

224. **Federal Home Loan Bank Board Report Under Section 415 of the
Competitive Equality Banking Act of 1987.** Washington, D.C.: Federal
Home Loan Bank Board, n.d. 64 p.

Goals, objectives, and a summary of operations are presented for the FHLBB,
FSLIC, FADA, ORPOS, and the District Banks. One section of the report
includes a combined FSLIC conservatorship's income and expense report.
Guidelines for third parties are given, including accountants, attorneys, private
investigators, appraisers, and FADA contractors.

225. **Report on the Prevention of Insolvencies Pursuant to Section 408 of
the Competitive Equality Banking Act of 1987.** Washington, D.C.: Federal
Home Loan Bank Board, n.d. 24 p.

CEBA required the FHLBB to make a report describing the steps taken to prevent thrift failures. The paper discusses how insolvencies occur touching on management deficiencies, economic conditions, and fraud and insider abuse. The prevention of insolvencies is tied to good management, strong capital, and steady profits. Supervisory tools and the regulatory environment are reviewed.

226. Special Report: The Competitive Equality Banking Act of 1987. Bethesda, MD: Mortgage Commentary, 1987. 62 p.

CEBA was enacted to bolster FSLIC with a $10.8 billion infusion. It also served as a vehicle for additional issues including: forbearance, permission to sell thrifts to financial and nonfinancial companies, and restriction of new activities for banks. This report presents an overview of each title of the Act.

RESOLUTION COST

227. **All in the Family: Government S&L Resolutions and Asset Sales in Metropolitan Houston.** Briefing Paper. Charlotte, NC: Southern Finance Project, August 18, 1992. 8 p.

RTC's sale of thrifts and their assets in Houston are costing taxpayers abnormally high fees. This paper is part of a large report being prepared by the Southern Finance Project related to commercial interests which are benefiting from the bailout. It is noted that the RTC resolved 584 S&Ls from its creation through yearend 1991. The report states that although buyers paid large prices for the core deposits of Houston thrifts, these deals will still cost taxpayers more than other deals. The Houston bailout cost 77 cents for every dollar of gross assets on the books, for thrifts sold nationwide the cost is only 33 cents for every dollar. This variance is attributed to the limited bidding for Houston thrifts, three institutions purchased more than three-quarters of all deposits in Harris County. The paper states that 19 percent of all surveyed properties in Texas sold for a fifth or less of their book value. Tables included reflect the largest buyers of RTC real estate in Texas and in the Houston MSA. Selected information on sale-to-book ratios is also given.

228. Barth, James R., Philip F. Bartholomew, and Peter J. Elmer. **The Cost of Liquidating Versus Selling Failed Thrift Institutions.** Research Paper No. 89-02. Washington, D.C.: Office of Thrift Supervision, November 1989. 21 p.

In 1988 there were 205 insolvent thrift resolutions. This paper assesses the cost savings, through assisted acquisitions instead of liquidations, for 179 institutions. The authors demonstrate that there are determinants of franchise value of insolvent S&Ls which make sales less costly than liquidations in some instances. References are provided.

229. Barth, James R., Philip F. Bartholomew, and Michael G. Bradley. **The Determinants of Thrift Institution Resolution Costs.** Research Paper No. 89-03. Washington, D.C.: Office of Thrift Supervision, November 1989. 84 p.

The cost imposed by resolved thrift institutions is examined for three separate time frames: 1980-1982, 1983-1984, and 1985-1988. The authors state that the comprehensiveness and quality of the data available allows them to address the econometric problems present in other studies. Included are numerous supporting tables, and references.

230. [Bartholomew, Philip F.] **The Cost of Forebearance During the Thrift Crisis.** CBO Staff Memorandum. Washington, D.C.: Congressional Budget Office, June 1991. 7 p. [2] p.

This analysis was prepared at the request of the Committee on Banking, Finance and Urban Affairs of the U.S. House of Representatives. An estimate is provided on the cost of delay in closing failed thrift institutions. Regulators have recently suggested forebearance to allow troubled depositories to restore themselves. The CBO estimates that this policy in the early part of the thrift crisis increased the bill for resolutions by about $66 billion. They further estimate that forebearance doubled the cost of the thrift bailout. The paper presents the methods used to arrive at these figures. Charts and graphs related to insolvencies and resolutions are included.

231. Carron, Andrew S. "The Thrift Industry Crisis of the 1980s: What Went Wrong?" In **The Future of the Thrift Industry**, pp. 23-35. San Francisco: Federal Home Loan Bank of San Francisco, 1989. 253 p. Proceedings of the Fourteenth Annual Conference, December 8-9, 1988.

A number of influences led to the thrift crisis, these are discussed, but the main focus of the paper is why the losses imposed high costs on the industry and the economy. Mr. Carron asserts that failures could have occurred without spillover effects. He identifies the conditions that resulted in institution problems becoming burdens for the whole economy. Contributors to the expansion of costs were net-worth depletion in the early 1980s, deposit insurance, inadequate examination and supervision, and failure to close institutions prior to insolvency. The author points out that signs of problems were evident 15 years earlier, and that widespread failures could have been avoided. He also declares that failure costs could have been held within existing resources. Panel presentations on this topic by Gillian Garcia, Stuart Greenbaum, and Edward Kane are included.

232.   Catastrophe in the Thrift Industry: A Study by the Office of
Congressman Charles E. Schumer.   Washington, D.C.:   Office of U.S.
Congressman Charles E. Schumer, 1988. 50 p.

Stating that the lack of information has hindered timely decision making, the
report asserts that FSLIC will be insolvent throughout the century. It points out
that the statistics released by the Bank Board understate thrift losses, and that the
Southwest Plan has added to the expense. The report emphasizes that the Bank
Board encouraged rapid and risky growth, and seriously underestimated the cost
of resolution. Also reported is that the Office of Management and Budget
opposed funding for supervisory resources. Many tables are presented
throughout in support of the text and extensive tables follow the text.

233. Causey, James R. An Independent Commentary Relating to the RTC's
Efforts to Reduce the Costs of the 1988-1989 FSLIC Transactions.
Washington, D.C.: Kaplan Associates, Inc., October 25, 1991. 23 p. [4] p.

FIRREA directed the RTC to modify or restructure FSLIC agreements in an
effort to save funds. This paper addresses issues related to the 199 institutions
placed into receivership during 1988-1989. There were 96 separate assistance
agreements with 15 in the Southwest Plan. The public policy issues are
reviewed as are RTC's efforts related to these issues. The RTC has estimated
cost savings from restructuring to be about $2 billion over the lives of the
agreements. The cost savings is questionable due to the amount of time
involved for the restructuring. The author points out that the affected S&Ls
may be left vulnerable to adverse consequences relating to the restructuring
which would result in a loss of profits. He asserts that failures could occur
which would be contrary to good public policy. Several issues related to this
and the overall cost to the government are explored, i.e. loss of income tax
revenues for laid off employees and additional costs related to unemployment
insurance, and the effect on the economy. Mr. Causey raises the question of the
effect of these actions on affordable housing and mortgage credit as industry
earnings are affected by lower FHLB System dividends due to prepayment of
advances. The author makes several recommendations, and points out that little
public benefit will result from continuing the process.

234.   Cole, Rebel A.   Agency Conflicts and Thrift Resolution Costs.
Financial Industry Studies Working Paper No. 3-90. Dallas, TX: Federal
Reserve Bank of Dallas, July 1990. 41 p.

Thrift resolutions that occurred between 1980-1988 are studied using a model
of thrift resolution costs as a function of agency conflicts. Agency conflicts in
three areas are examined: shareholders and managers maximize their

institution's returns through high-risk projects at the expense of unsecured creditors and government agencies; conflicts lead managers to maximize their personal returns; and agency conflicts lead parties within the FHLB System "to maximize the personal returns from their positions at the expense of the FSLIC . . . and the public interest." These conflicts increase resolution costs. The costs under various scenarios are studied. "The analysis finds that thrift resolution costs are positively related to measures of capital-loss coverage . . . . " The author offers policy recommendations. Four pages of references are included.

235. Cole, Rebel A., Robert A. Eisenbeis, and Joseph A. McKenzie. **Excess Returns and Sources of Value in FSLIC-Assisted Acquisitions of Troubled Thrifts**. FIS No. 1-89. Dallas, TX: Federal Reserve Bank of Dallas, December 1989. 32 p.

Possible incentives for the FHLBB to underestimate the costs of resolutions from 1980-1988 are presented. This is followed by a study of gains by assisted thrift acquisitions versus unassisted acquisitions. The data and methodology are described, followed by the empirical results. References are included and tables provide supporting data.

236. Cole, Rebel A. and Robert A. Eisenbeis. "Value Creation and Excess Returns in FSLIC-Assisted Acquisitions of Troubled Thrifts." In **Banking System Risk: Charting a New Course**, pp. 457-476. Chicago: Federal Reserve Bank of Chicago, 1989. 604 p. The 25th Annual Conference on Bank Structure and Competition, May 3-5, 1989.

The authors were with the Federal Reserve Bank of Dallas and the University of North Carolina at Chapel Hill respectively. Their introduction asserts that, "Since FSLIC was charged with resolving cases at minimum cost to the insurance fund and was short of cash, it had incentives to shift as much of the cost of assistance as possible to the Treasury and the taxpayer in the form of reduced federal income taxes paid by acquirers." FSLIC rushed to conclude deals by December 31, 1988 to retain the full tax exemptions. The authors studied returns to shareholders of thrifts engaged in assisted mergers, and returns to thrifts engaged in unassisted transactions. They determine that FSLIC assistance resulted in increases in returns of 8-9% over a three-week period following the acquisitions. References and charts are included.

237. Cooper, Mary H. **S & L Bailout: Assessing the Impact**. Editorial Research Reports. Washington, D.C.: Congressional Quarterly, Inc., 1990. [15] p.

The economic aspect of the bailout and its impact on the deficit is examined. Included is a breakdown by Edward W. Hill listing which states will gain and lose money from the bailout process. An "outlook" for the financial industry is presented.

238. DeGennaro, Ramon P. and James B. Thomson. **Capital Forbearance and Thrifts: An Ex Post Examination of Regulatory Gambling.** Working Paper 9209. Cleveland, OH: Federal Reserve Bank of Cleveland, 1992. 44 p.

The authors analyze the direct costs of regulatory forbearance of insolvent FSLIC-insured institutions. At the end of the 1970s there were 996 FSLIC-insured thrifts that did not meet capital standards. The authors compare the estimated cost of resolving the insolvencies at the end of the 1970s with the actual resolution costs for those institutions closed by 7-31-92. They conclude, "We find that taxpayers lost the forbearance bet, as the present value of future closure costs is more than double the cost of prompt intervention." References are included.

239. **The Economic Effects of the Savings & Loan Crisis.** [Washington, D.C.]: Congressional Budget Office, January 1992. 63 p.

The CBO was requested to access the damage to the economy caused by the budgetary costs associated with the S&L failures. The summary to the report states "all of the economic effects of the losses . . . suffered are difficult to untangle." The study points out that borrowing to finance the resolutions has no negative effect on the budget, but the reduction in savings and capital accumulation reduces GNP. The impacts of the budget obligations are presented. The economic effects are first analyzed and estimates are given with the effects projected through 2007. Forecasts are provided through 2010.

240. Ely, Bert. **Crime Accounts for Only 3% of the Cost of the S&L Mess.** Alexandria, VA: Ely & Co., Inc., July 19, 1990. 7 p.

Mr. Ely evaluates the cost of the S&L debacle. He states that interest costs comprise about 39% of the losses. About 19% of the cost can be attributed to "price deflation, bad lending, and real estate deterioration." The failure to dispose of failed institutions in 1983 contributes about 17% to the current cleanup costs. Other components are losses on junk bonds, excess interest paid by insolvent S&Ls, deterioration of the deposit franchise in insolvent thrifts, and excessive cost of FSLIC's 1988 deals. The author concludes that actual crime composes only 3% of the total cost of the cleanup.

241. Ettleson, Sherry and Thomas Hilliard. **Crime and Punishment in the S&L Industry: The Bush Administration's Anemic War on S&L Fraud.** Washington, D.C.: Public Citizen's Congress Watch, June 1990. 23 p.

An analysis of Justice Department records, regulatory agency statistics, and congressional testimony lead the authors to conclude that the S&L criminals will "get away with it." Charts and tables present figures related to fraud and enforcement. The reasons for the recovery problems are discussed and recommendations given.

242. Gatti, James F. and Ronald W. Spahr. **Evaluating the Costs of FSLIC Case Resolution.** Research Paper No. 149. Washington, D.C.: Federal Home Loan Bank Board, September 1988. 25 p.

The cost to FSLIC of handling failed thrifts is evaluated in this study as are the problems inherent in each resolution method. Models are developed for the evaluation with the goal being to optimize the allocation of limited resources to resolve thrifts. The authors suggest standardizing assistance packages and eliminating post-bid negotiations. They suggest that use of their models will simplify the structure and evaluation of bids.

243. Hill, Edward W. **Federal Savings and Loan Bailout Regional Economic Development on a Grand Scale.** Cleveland, OH: Cleveland State University, 1989. [7] p.

Professor Hill asserts that 36 states are helping bail out the problems of 14 states. He calculated the economic impact as a result of this transfer of wealth. Tables provide financial data.

244. Laughlin, Keith, Mary Weaver, and Bob Kelley. **Stuck With the Tab: The Regional Implications of the Savings and Loan Bail-Out.** Washington, D.C.: The Northeast-Midwest Congressional Coalition, 1989. 14 p.

Using tables and charts this report shows the 1988 FSLIC case resolution cost by state and related state economic data. The point of the paper is to demonstrate that the Northeast-Midwest region is shouldering 47% of the S&L tax burden while its thrifts were responsible for less than 10% of the cost.

245. Laughlin, Keith and Mary Weaver. **Stuck With the Tab Part 2: The Nightmare Continues.** Washington, D.C.: The Northeast-Midwest Congressional Coalition, 1990. 16 p.

Focusing on the inequity of the tax burden relating to the thrift bailout, this report states that the Northeast-Midwest region shoulders 47% of the nation's tax burden, but is responsible for only 10% of the insolvent thrifts. The report reviews the S&L disaster while pointing out that this region relies on federal discretionary funding for revitalization, and that it is contributing more than its share to the resolution costs.

246. Payne, Roslyn B. "Nonperforming Assets: Observations and Lessons Learned." In **Thrift Financial Performance and Capital Adequacy**, pp. 57-64. San Francisco, CA: Federal Home Loan Bank of San Francisco, 1987. 187 p. Proceedings of the Twelfth Annual Conference, December 11-12, 1986.

Speaking as President and CEO of the Federal Asset Disposition Association (FADA), Ms. Payne explains its creation, purpose, and role. She notes that one half of the FHLBB's supervisory cases are experiencing asset-performance problems with ADC and participation loans. Condominium conversions and time-share projects are present in 13% of the problem institutions. The use of brokered money to fund these projects has resulted in billions of dollars of losses. FADA's job is to manage and dispose of FSLIC's portfolio of troubled assets. FADA has identified the causes of problems as: poor underwriting procedures, problem participation loans, lack of management systems, and fraud.

MERGERS, ACQUISITIONS, AND CONVERSIONS

247. Federal Home Loan Bank Board. **Purchasing an Insolvent Savings Institution Through the Federal Savings and Loan Insurance Corporation.** Washington, D.C.: Federal Home Loan Bank Board, 1988. [57] p.

Background information on the Bank System and the advantages of a savings institution charter are provided in this paper. Investor qualification requirements, financial assistance programs, tax considerations, regulatory waivers and forebearances, and accounting aspects are explained. Included is a sample proposal and forms required for proposal submittal.

248. Kohers, Theodor and Dennis Bialaszewski. **The Impact of Recent Merger Trends on the Savings and Loan Industry.** Atlanta, GA: Financial Management Association, 1983. 18 p. Presented at the annual meeting.

In response to financial difficulties "regulators have rushed to facilitate mergers of weak institutions with sound ones," from 1981-1982 the industry "has shrunk by 20 percent as a result of merger activity." This study attempts to determine to what extent the mergers of 1981-1982 contributed to changes in the industry. For this period the ownership, charter, size, and major characteristics of institutions is studied. The research data, methodology, and results are presented. Some of the changes between year-end 1982 and year-end 1980 are: reduced investments in single family homes, asset diversification, borrowings from sources other than FHLBB increased by 80%, CDs over $100,000 increased by 65%, capital positions continued to deteriorate, net worth/total asset ratio dropped by 20%, key measures of profitability declined, and expense variables increased. The authors conclude that the consolidations have had a positive impact on the remaining industry, and that "the recent merger trend can

be considered to have contributed to an improvement in the industry."
References are given.

249. Mergers Involving Savings and Loan Associations: Implications for Future Activity and Antitrust Issues. Washington, D.C.: Kaplan, Smith and Associates, Inc., April 1981. 202 p.

The FHLBB contracted with Kaplan, Smith to perform a study of mergers, and to make recommendations to the Board regarding this issue. FHLBB merger policies and procedures were evaluated. Future trends in merger activity were addressed. This study found "evidence that synergy is realized by merging S&Ls." They found that there are similar risk characteristics for merging and non-merging institutions. Merging associations held greater proportions of mortgage loans than non-merging institutions. The study strongly supports a pro-merger stance for the FHLBB. Specific policy recommendations and objectives are included. The "antitrust dilemma" is explored in detail. Eighty-five tables are included illustrating the analysis conducted. References are given.

250. Mingo, John J. "Short-Run Structural Solutions to the Problems of Thrift Institutions." In **The Future of the Thrift Industry**, pp. 81-106. Conference Series No. 24. Boston: Federal Reserve Bank of Boston, [1982]. 187 p. Proceedings of a Conference held October 1981.

Two possible solutions to thrift problems are to give aid until interest rates drop, or to merge thrifts out of existence. This paper analyzes the conditions which would make assisted mergers less expensive than subsidies to the deposit insurance fund. Further, the paper discusses the public costs/benefits outside of the insuring agencies. The perspective is from the FDIC insurance of mutual savings banks, but the author notes the conclusions would apply to all thrifts. It is emphasized that mergers would not affect the supply of mortgage money, and that competition would not be significantly affected.

251. The Thrift Industry in 1985. Commercial Law and Practice Course Handbook Series No. 370. [New York]: Practising Law Institute, 1985. 1036 p.

Although many presentations are included in this handbook they primarily fall under three broad topics: financing alternatives, conversions, and mergers and acquisitions. Among those making presentations were Thomas Vartanian, Ernest Leff, and Richard Kneipper. Additionally, Robert M. Kurucza presented "Registration of Thrifts as Broker-Dealers." Reproductions of articles and ruling letters are included in the manual.

252. Vartanian, Thomas P. **Takeover Case Studies and Recent Regulatory Developments**. Washington, D.C.: National Council of Savings Institutions, 1987. [171] p. Lawyers Seminar, January 25-28, 1987.

Mr. Vartanian is former General Counsel of the FHLBB and FSLIC. The seminar proceedings contain two articles, one related to mergers, and the second on conversion to a stock institution. Also included are various FHLBB opinion letters and articles related to "The Definition of 'Voting Stock'". A lock-up transaction chart is presented next. Reproductions of several press releases related to "Shareholder's Rights Plans" are included. The next section presents FHLBB memos R41c, SP-57, and SP-68, and articles related to asset quality. "Berlin Wall" developments compose section seven, with excerpts from a proxy statement, and a FHLBB general counsel letter. The final portion of this booklet contains information related to the "Business Judgment Rule and Director and Officer Issues".

FAILED THRIFTS

253. Adams, James Ring. **The Big Fix: Inside the S&L Scandal.** New York: John Wiley & Sons, Inc., 1990. 308 p. index.

In telling the story of the S&L debacle, the journalist author includes a major dose of political corruption and betrayal. The story of old line solid thrifts sold to big time gamblers is told. Players included are the Butcher brothers, Herman Beebe, Spencer Blain, Linton Bowman, Ray Corona, Don Dixon, Craig Hall, Charles Keating, Bert Lance, Marvin Warner, and Jim Wright. The regulators, their roles and personalities, are part of the story which includes the OCC, FDIC, FRB, FSLIC, and the FHLBB. The 1980 S&L ties to the 1970s "rent a bank" scandal personalities are mentioned, as are other details. Charts illustrate the various connections between the key players. This book received positive reviews when it was released and is a good vehicle for becoming familiar with the names involved in this phase of the industry.

254. Bisenius, Donald J., R. Dan Brumbaugh, Jr., and Ronald C. Rogers. **Insolvent Thrift Institutions, Agency Issues, and the Management Consignment Program.** Research Paper No. 141. Washington, D.C.: Federal Home Loan Bank Board, October 1986. 22 p.

An overview of the Management Consignment Program is presented in this paper. The program was created in April 1985 to reduce FSLIC losses by taking control of the decision-making process of the institution rather than closing it. The paper discusses agency issues, the effectiveness of MCP and its future. References are included.

255. Cole, Rebel A. **Thrift Resolution Activity: Historical Overview and Implications.** Financial Industry Studies. Dallas, TX: Federal Reserve Bank of Dallas, May 1990. 12 p.

Thrift resolutions completed in the 1980s and their public policy implications are examined in this article. It is noted that there were two "waves" of resolutions. The first from 1980-1982 which resulted from interest rate spread problems. Asset quality problems created the second "wave" of resolutions in the late 1980s. Charts and tables compare Texas resolutions with the nation. The author also scrutinizes the returns to thrift acquirers, and states that they were overcompensated. He concludes that complex mergers involving open-ended assistance are more costly than whole-bank and clean-bank transactions. References are given.

256. Crockett, John H. **On the Good Bank/Bad Bank Restructuring of Failed Thrifts.** Research Working Paper No. 129. Washington, D.C.: Federal Home Loan Bank Board, May 1987. 31 p.

One of the new strategies developed by the insurance agencies to respond to failing institutions is the good bank/bad bank restructuring. A reorganization of asset holdings is involved with significant assets or groups of assets removed from the portfolio. Another part of restructuring is changes in the composition of claims against the firm. The FSLIC restructuring model separates the "good" assets from the "bad" assets, they are managed separately. Restructuring allows FSLIC to reduce losses by increasing the value of its equity position in failed institutions. This paper examines restructuring to "clarify the sources of its likely benefits and costs." The author notes that this strategy has been used by commercial banks as well. The second section of the paper discusses thrift institution failures and ways of handling the failures. Thrift restructuring is examined in the next section of the paper, which notes that the first asset-backed transfer of accounts was in August 1985 involving Westside FS&L of Seattle. A chart provides information on the eleven asset-backed transfers which occurred in 1985-1986. The author examines the parallels between thrift and corporate restructuring. Positive aspects of restructuring are improvement of the net cash flow position due to more efficient management of assets; management specialization of the differing activities required from a solvent thrift and an insolvent one; and an increase in bidders and higher bids, because of the confidence level when bad assets are removed. The author notes there are a number of variables which have not been examined that affect restructuring advantages. References are listed.

257. **Fact Sheet.** Washington, D.C.: Resolution Trust Corporation, 1992. v.p.

The RTC releases this information on a weekly basis. The **Fact Sheet** reflects the total S&Ls which are enrolled in the regulatory oversight program. Presented are aggregate numbers by state. Also listed by state are individual institution names, total assets and deposits. This information has been published since 1990.

258. Gibson, William E. "A Practical Perspective on Thrift Difficulties." In **Merging Commercial and Investment Banking**, pp. 332-336. Chicago: Federal Reserve Bank of Chicago, [1988]. 630 p. Proceedings of the 23rd Annual Conference on Bank Structure and Competition, May 6-8, 1987.

The author offers observations about the "Phoenix" program from the perspective of a chairman of one and a director of another institution in the program. The Phoenix program began Labor Day weekend of 1982. Initially the problems of three New York thrifts were addressed. Troubled thrifts in a market area were merged into lead thrifts. Later three other New York institutions were merged into one of the Phoenixes, and four additional Phoenix institutions were created. The merged institutions had credit quality problems, but the main problem was interest rate spread. Management was seen as capable at these institutions but unable to deal with the high interest rates and specialization in long-term mortgages. The problems were too great for FSLIC to handle. The mergers were aimed to strengthen management, eliminate duplications, and cut costs. The problems were worked though "with some FSLIC assistance, mostly covering the present value of the losses up to 1982." FSLIC ended the Phoenix status in 1986.

259. Gup, Benton. **Bank Fraud: Exposing the Hidden Threat to Financial Institutions.** Rolling Meadows, IL: Bankers Publishing Co., 1990. 247 p.

Using articles, house reports, and other sources, the author compiled information on major frauds at financial institutions. He lists types of fraud, and specifies institutions and individuals. Fraud at banks, thrifts, and insurance companies is covered. Mr. Gup also suggests ways to prevent future occurrences of fraud and insider abuse. Appendices contain sample loan policies and "red flags" as indicators of possible fraud. Sources are listed throughout the text, and at the end of the book.

260. Horvitz, Paul M. "Assessing the Management Consignment Program." In **Merging Commercial and Investment Banking**, pp. 337-340. Chicago: Federal Reserve Bank of Chicago, [1988]. 630 p. Proceedings of the 23rd Annual Conference on Bank Structure and Competition, May 6-8, 1987.

Lacking the resources to implement other solutions, FSLIC has used the MCP program out of necessity. FSLIC takes over an insolvent institution, appoints a new board, and contracts for management. FDIC has referred to this arrangement as a "bridge bank". The MCP allows time for FSLIC to get the institution's books in order, and for potential bidders to evaluate the institution. Mr. Horvitz touches on MCPs from a management and director viewpoint. He points out that lack of funds has led to long delays in resolution of the MCP thrifts. He further states that "the program has considerable merit as a temporary means of handling problems . . . ."

261. McCulloch, J. Huston. "The Ohio S&L Crisis in Retrospect: Implications for the Current Federal Deposit Insurance Crisis." In **Merging Commercial and Investment Banking**, pp. 230-251. Chicago: Federal Reserve Bank of Chicago, [1988]. 630 p. Proceedings of the 23rd Annual Conference on Bank Structure and Competition, May 6-8, 1987.

The author begins by describing the demise of the Ohio Deposit Guarantee Fund, which was a result of Home State Savings' involvement with ESM Government Securities. The "runs" on the state's thrifts are discussed and the national thrift crisis is reviewed. Mr. McCulloch discusses how thrifts can operate in a sound manner by reducing interest rate risk. He then examines the lessons to be learned from the Ohio experience. References are given.

262. Maggin, Donald L. **Bankers, Builders, Knaves, and Thieves: The $300 Million Scam at ESM**. Chicago: Contemporary Books, 1989. 308 p. index.

In the early 1980s only five states allowed thrifts to "opt out" of FSLIC insurance, Ohio was one of those states. Home State Savings Bank of Cincinnati and 68 other institutions were insured by the Ohio Deposit Guarantee Fund. ODGF's capital requirements were less stringent than those of FSLIC and its assets were only $136 million. This book tells the story of the ESM scam which led to the failure of Ohio's second largest S&L and the closing of 68 other S&Ls. Detailed in the story are the negotiations to obtain FSLIC coverage for state S&Ls and the state legislative workings. Major players in this story are Marvin Warner, Joe Gomez, Alan Novick, and George Mead. Also described are the efforts to win recoveries for the fraud victims. This is an interesting account of the debacle caused by the ESM fraud.

263. Mayer, Martin. **The Greatest-Ever Bank Robbery: The Collapse of the Savings and Loan Industry**. N.Y.: Charles Scribner's Sons, 1990. 354 p. index.

Discussing specific institutions, and those involved with the institutions, this book tells the story of the S&L industry demise. Mr. Mayer tells what happened and explains how it happened. Among institutions discussed are Vernon, Western, and Lincoln S&Ls. Jim Wright, Charles Keating, Richard Pratt, and Danny Wall are among the many individuals discussed.

264. O'Shea, James. **The Daisy Chain: How Borrowed Billions Sank a Texas S&L.** N.Y.: Pocket Books, 1991. 351 p. index.

A journalist for the Chicago Tribune, Mr. O'Shea states that he depended heavily on court testimony and interviews to write this book. This is the story of Vernon S&L and Donald R. Dixon. Written in a very readable fashion the book tells of Mr. Dixon's purchase of Vernon and his elaborate spending, often referred to as the "looting" of Vernon Savings and Loan. The subsequent government take over of Vernon is detailed. A chapter describes Representative Jim Wright's role in the S&L scandal. Extensive author's notes list sources of information used in writing the book.

265. Pilzer, Paul Zane and Robert Deitz. **Other People's Money: The Inside Story of the S&L Mess.** New York: Simon and Schuster, 1989. 269 p. index.

Mr. Pilzer, a partner of an investment company, wrote this book with a journalist, Robert Deitz. At the time the book was written both gentlemen lived in Dallas. The book begins with an overview of the banking system, why savings was important to the U.S., and the deregulation of S&Ls. Three chapters present general coverage of the situation in Texas and California, mentioning institutions and key players. Regulatory inadequacies are covered, as are the politicians' part in the story. A chapter is devoted to the underestimation of the cost of the crisis, which includes discussion of the Southwest Plan. The author also discusses possible solutions to the S&L problem. This title presents a broad overview of the major components of the crisis. A selected bibliography is included.

266. Pizzo, Stephen, Mary Fricker, and Paul Muolo. **Inside Job: The Looting of America's Savings and Loans.** New York: McGraw-Hill Publishing Co., 1989. 443 p. index.

All three authors were newspaper reporters when this book was written. This title received much publicity at the time of publication because of the authors' contention of "mob" involvement in the S&L frauds. In the introduction the authors state that their investigations repeatedly found ties between thrift failures, leading them to the conclusion that a network of looting existed. Their

investigations "uncovered mobsters, arms dealers, drug money launderers, and
. . . wheeler-dealers." The index consists of fifteen pages of individual and
institution names, some seen in other exposes, with many additions. The
appendices include "The Comptroller Report on Herman K. Beebe", and a
FSLIC memorandum describing a meeting with Senators on behalf of Charles
Keating. Extensive notes support the text. An intriguing story is woven by the
authors.

**267. Report of the National Council of Savings Institutions Task Force on
Operating Limits for Capital-Impaired Institutions.** Washington, D.C.:
National Council of Savings Institutions, August 4, 1988. 5 p.

FSLIC is allowing capital-impaired institutions to continue to operate because
it lacks the resources to dispose of the institutions. This penalizes healthy
institutions in two ways: unfair competition with insolvent institutions; and the
cost of the insolvencies to the industry. The National Council of Savings
Institutions created a task force to review the growth of insolvent institutions,
and the effect on competition. The task force adopted these recommendations:
prohibit insolvent institutions from making new loans or acquiring new
investments; shift supervision of hopelessly insolvents from District Banks to
Bank Board; restrict the growth of capital impaired institutions; and structure
FSLIC-assisted acquisitions and mergers on a risk-averse basis.

268. Robinson, Michael A. **Overdrawn: The Bailout of American Savings.**
New York: Dutton, 1990. 303 p.

In mid-1984 American S&LA of Stockton, California was the nation's largest
thrift. It was owned by Financial Corporation of America, and was growing by
$1 billion a month. The institution was plagued by unsound loans, and was
suffering a run of withdrawals. Mr. Robinson, a Pulitzer Prize writing
nominee, traces the history of the demise of American. Personalities are woven
into the story, including regulators and the regulated. Charlie Knapp, owner of
FCA and a tremendous risk taker, was in trouble with the FHLBB as well as
the SEC. The collapse of American threatened a national financial disaster.
The story includes details of the regulator's role in averting collapse, those
courted to purchase the institution, and the sale to the Bass group. The author
made extensive use of interviews in the story construction.

269. Rodrigues, Jess A. **Power Above the Law.** San Ramon, CA: Presse
Foreward, Inc., 1990. 204 p. index.

The story of Saratoga Savings and Loan Association, located in California, is
told by its owner. Mr. Rodrigues asserts that regulatory incompetence resulted

in the closure of hundreds of S&Ls rather than actual failure of the institutions. This book was written to present "the other side" of the story. The years from the founding of the institution through its government seizure, as well as Mr. Rodrigues' efforts for relief, are traced in the book.

270. **RTC Review.** Washington, D.C.: Resolution Trust Corporation, 1992. v.p.

The **Review** contains information related to institutions closed, asset inventory, asset sales, and dollar amounts related to resolutions. This newsletter has been published since 1990. A separate publication, RTC news releases, lists information related to institutions as they are placed into the conservatorship program.

271. Sterngold, James. **Burning Down the House: How Greed, Deceit, and Bitter Revenge Destroyed E. F. Hutton.** New York: Summit Books, 1990. 305 p. index.

The story of Hutton and its fall from glory is a complex story involving many companies and personalities. Hutton's business relationship with First American Mortgage Company (FAMCO) is discussed. FAMCO, operating from Maryland, had second-mortgage origination offices in the South. The company's mortgage rates were usurious and the points were often 30% of the mortgage. In some instances the borrower interest was 100%. These loans were often purchased by ailing thrifts in an effort to bolster their sagging returns. Hutton was an intermediary for these loans. FAMCO often sold the same loan three or four times. Another thrift tie-in to this story relates to J.B. Haralson. Hutton was the advisor for Mercury S&L and Ben Milam S&L, owned by Haralson, when they purchased mortgage banking units from Orbanco and Baldwin-United. Hutton earned a $5.8 million fee and helped Haralson hide the fact that he was actually "fronting" for George Aubin. Aubin had been restricted by Texas regulators from involvement with Texas financial institutions. Ultimately Orbanco and Baldwin-United sued Hutton when the truth was learned. Hutton was also hired to locate a buyer for Mercury and Ben Milam when Haralson was forced by regulators to sell the thrifts. Due to the large commissions earned from doing business with Aubin, Hutton's relationship with these two men was tangled, and ultimately led to large losses.

272. Wilmsen, Steven K. **Silverado: Neil Bush and the Savings & Loan Scandal.** Washington, D. C.: National Press Books, 1991. 207 p. index.

The author, a financial reporter in Denver, covered the Silverado scandal in the local press. He discovered Neil Bush's business ties to Silverado's borrowers. Mr. Wilmsen writes of the delay in closing Silverado until after the 1988 election. This is the story of Silverado S&L and the people involved in its rise and fall.

1988 RESOLUTIONS

273. Barth, James R., Philip F. Bartholomew, and Carol J. Labich. "Moral Hazard and the Thrift Crisis: An Analysis of 1988 Resolutions." In **Banking System Risk: Charting a New Course**, pp. 344-384. Chicago: Federal Reserve Bank of Chicago, 1989. 604 p. The 25th Annual Conference on Bank Structure and Competition, May 3-5, 1989.

The three authors were with the Office of Policy and Economic Research at the FHLBB. The first part of the paper documents the magnitude of the crisis. Charts as well as discussion present numbers and percentages for loss related facts. Charts also show the regional distribution of resolution costs, and a comparison of the 1930s and 1980s. It is noted that failures in the 1980s, with deposit insurance, generated greater losses than in the 1930s without deposit insurance. Causes of the crisis, compose the third section of the paper. The causes are identified as: rigid institutional design, high and volatile interest rates, deterioration in asset quality, deregulation, fraudulent practices, and the moral hazard of deposit insurance. The discussion is concluded with this statement, "In sum, federal deposit insurance is a cause of the current thrift crisis." The next section reviews the extent to which regulators contributed to the crisis through delays in closing insolvent thrifts, required capital levels, interest rates, and resolutions. Charts and discussion relate that the composition of institution's portfolios do change as capital deteriorates. Also, that direct investments, and acquisition and development loans do have a significant effect on resolution costs. The authors state that "insufficient capital and the lack of a timely closure rule were major causes of the thrift crisis." References are provided at the end of the article.

274. **Consolidation and Capital Are Key To Success of FHLBB Southwest Plan.** News Release 88-30. Washington, D.C.: Federal Home Loan Bank Board, February 3, 1988. 4 p.

The Southwest Plan is announced with this news release. Mergers are projected to reduce the total number of Texas thrifts from 281 to 160-180. The release states, "Wall estimated the up-front cost of eliminating the negative net worth of Texas thrifts at between $6 and $7 billion."

275. **Deregulation, Economics and Fraud Are Factors in Texas Thrift Story.** News Release 88-31. Washington, D.C.: Federal Home Loan Bank Board, February 3, 1988. 16 p.

This news release discusses the Southwest Plan, stating that the recapitalization funds "will provide much of the financial assistance required to execute the plan." Success of the plan depends on consolidation of Texas thrifts. "The Southwest Plan calls for dividing Texas into 14 thrift regions . . . ." The objectives of the plan are to cut operating costs and reduce the "premium they have been paying for funds." A fact sheet and several charts are included.

276. **FHLBB'S Southwest Plan Launched: Five Texas Thrifts Consolidated.** News Release 88-89. Washington, D.C.: Federal Home Loan Bank Board, May 13, 1988. 4 p.

Four acquisitions to launch the Southwest Plan were announced. Coastal Banc Savings acquired southeast Texas thrifts. The deposits and assets of Alliance S&LA, Colorado County FS&LA, Security S&LA, and Cameron County SA were acquired. The consolidation increased Coastal's assets from $70 million to $600 million.

277. Haregot, Seyoum A., et al. **Let's Make a Deal: An Analysis of the 1988 Savings and Loan Bailouts and the Federal Campaign Contributions of Associated Individuals and Political Action Committees.** Washington, D.C.: Center for Study of Responsive Law, July 1991. [147] p.

The "sweetheart" deals of 1988 benefitted the acquirers of some 220 thrifts. These deals included the "Southwest Plan" thrifts. Government subsidies and tax breaks were promised to the buyers, which included Robert Bass, Ronald Perelman, and William Simon. It has been estimated that the buyers received $78 in assets and benefits for every $1 invested. This report examines the deals and why they were made, the campaign contributions of acquiring entities, and lists the recipients of the contributions. Tables and charts present the following information: major shareholders of acquiring entities with more than $10,000 in political contributions (name, institution, amount); PAC contributions (affiliated with acquirers); beneficiaries of contributions (names, state, party, amount); acquiring entity, contribution, cost to government; transaction information for 96 deals includes financial data, and shareholder, officer/director names; and contributions to political campaigns by shareholders, officers and directors. The study recommends an investigation into the deals, release of all government information related to the deals, and campaign finance reform.

278. Kormendi, Roger C., et al. **Crisis Resolution in the Thrift Industry: A Mid America Institute Report**. Boston: Kluwer Academic Publishers, 1989. 84 p.

The Senate Banking Committee suggested to the FHLBB that it obtain an independent study related to thrift resolutions, especially the "December deals." The Bank Board contacted the Mid America Institute, which agreed to do the study from an academic perspective. The report does not address the issues of budgetary or political constraints. The focus is on the 1988 resolutions and the lessons to be learned from them which might facilitate future resolutions. The panel evaluated their impact on the U.S. government's liabilities and possible future impact. The study's analysis suggests that the government's costs for assisted acquisitions may be substantially higher than the FSLIC's estimates. Preliminary analysis indicates that the "December deals" and the "Texas deals" were no more or less costly than other assisted acquisitions. However, the tax benefit rebates in essence shifted cost from one agency to another. The study of the bidding and negotiation process included information on assistance agreements and contractual terms. The FSLIC bid methodology was evaluated, and the cost of solutions examined. Tables present information on the cost of solution and benefits accruing to the acquirer, the 10 highest resolutions by value of cost, evaluation of Bass bid, and cost savings of December vs. Non-December deals. The panel concludes by suggesting the development of a "clean assistance package" to replace the other assistance packages. The Clean Assistance Package would streamline the bidding process by fixing the contract terms prior to bidding, require tax benefit rebates to FSLIC, exclude all special forbearances, and would not receive warrants as part of agreements. References are included.

279. Mid America Institute Task Force on the Thrift Crisis. **Crisis Resolution in the Thrift Industry: Beyond the December Deals**. n.p.: University of Michigan, 1989. 106 p.

The Senate Banking Committee suggested an independent study of the Bank Board and FSLIC. To this end the Bank Board approached the Institute to conduct the study. The study was to focus on the "December deals," especially the related tax considerations. The majority of the study covers the FSLIC acquisition bidding and negotiation process in 1988; an analysis of the methodology for evaluating bids; and a review of the FSLIC's cost. The acquisition and negotiation process explains the Southwest Plan strategy and analyzes the contractual terms of the agreements. The key recommendation was for a "Clean Assistance Package," which would lessen the incentive and valuation problems, and streamline the negotiation process.

280. Root, Stuart D. **Southwest Plan Objectives and Means for Achieving Them.** [Washington, D.C.: Kaplan Associates], October 21, 1991. 6 p.

Development of the pre-RTC policies, and the RTC response to the 1988 FSLIC transactions are reviewed in this paper. It asserts that it is imprudent public policy to write down or sell assets when real estate values are low. The author advocates a return to a workout approach. The Southwest plan objectives and the means for achieving them are described in detail. The objectives listed are: stem the losses, reduce the "Texas Premium," attract new management, and attract new capital. The results are reviewed noting that the losses were not stopped but deferred. The author also points out that testimony in 1990 indicated that the Southwest Plan deals were no more expensive than other 1988 deals. A footnote states that this paper is "from an Appendix to a manuscript entitled: 'From the Eye of the S&L Storm: An Insider's View of Collapse and a Failed Recovery - Or, All Pretty Heady for a Boy from Chagrin Falls.'"

281. **Southwest Plan Leads Wave of Thrift Acquisitions.** [New York]: Ernst & Whinney, 1988. 17 p.

FSLIC activities are summarized in this pamphlet. The benefits to investors, and financial and tax considerations related to thrift acquisitions is discussed.

282. Vartanian, Thomas P., et al. **Summary of FSLIC Resolutions Under the Southwest Plan and Other Significant Assisted Transactions.** Washington, D.C.: Fried, Frank, Harris, Shriver & Jacobson, October 20, 1988. [32] p.

Mr. Vartanian has served as General Counsel of the FHLBB and FSLIC. In chart form he provides financial information related to Southwest Plan case resolutions and other FSLIC assisted transactions since May 1988. Included is the amount of the FSLIC note, term and interest rate of note, acquirer's capital infusion, term of assistance agreement, covered assets yield maintenance, capital loss coverage, FSLIC equity, tax benefits, prenuptial net worth, and other features of the transactions.

FAILURE ANALYSIS
AND PREDICTION

283. Balderston, Frederick E. **Analysis of the Viability of S&L Firms.**
Center for Real Estate and Urban Economics Working Paper Series No. 82-54.
Berkeley, CA: University of California, September 1982. 18 p.

Using computer generated projections the future viability of S&Ls is examined.
Three alternative interest-rate scenarios from 1982-1985 are used to determine
the number of S&Ls that will survive. The semi-annual financial reports filed
with the FHLBB by thrifts forms the basis for this exercise. The scenarios are
for continuously high interest rates, continuously falling rates, and a cyclic
scenario. Factored in are assumptions of no growth or decline in savings
deposits and growth coordinated with each scenario. Using these projections it
would be possible to ascertain each institution's future prospects.

284. Balderston, Frederick E. **Deterioration Processes in Troubled Financial
Institutions and Their Implications for Public Policy.** Center for Real Estate
and Urban Economics Working Paper Series No. 85-104. Berkeley, CA:
University of California, 1985. 31 p.

Deterioration processes are examined on two levels: first, the slow, steady
deterioration which gives management, stockholders, and regulators time to seek
reversals; and secondly, the rapid deterioration experienced both by no-growth
and rapid growth institutions. These are discussed in the context of asset risks
by direct investment, loans to one borrower, and conflict of interest in lending.
A financial firm model was constructed to illustrate the elements of managerial
policy and market response. Also constructed was a "collapse model" for slow
and fast deterioration. The author calls for public policy which will "motivate
stockholders and managers toward greater prudence in the operation of the
financial enterprise." He also suggests that net worth reserves should be

"maintained continuously at the required levels or should be replenished at quarterly or monthly intervals." A short list of references is included.

285. Barth, James R., Dan Brumbaugh, Jr., and Daniel Sauerhaft. **Failure Costs of Government-Regulated Financial Firms: The Case of Thrift Institutions.** Research Working Paper No. 123. Washington D.C.: Federal Home Loan Bank Board, October 1986. 40 p.

This paper focuses on determining the likelihood that an institution will fail and the cost to the insurance fund for the failure. It examines the importance of timely closing of the institution, and develops a model which describes the relationship between market-value to book-value net worth and failure costs. References are provided.

286. Barth, James R., Philip F. Bartholomew, and Carol J. Labich. **Moral Hazard and the Thrift Crisis: An Analysis of 1988 Resolutions.** Research Paper No. 160. Washington, D.C.: Federal Home Loan Bank Board, May 1989. 47 p.

The magnitude of the crisis is documented and the causes are discussed in this paper. The focus is the role of deposit insurance in the crisis. Charts and tables present industry resolution information from 1980-1988, including regional distribution. References are found at the end of the paper.

287. Barth, James R., et al. "Thrift-Institution Failures: Causes and Policy Issues." In **Proceedings of a Conference on Bank Structure and Competition,** pp. 184-216. Chicago: Federal Reserve Bank of Chicago, 1985. 641 p.

A historical perspective on thrift and FSLIC problems is presented by the authors, including a discussion of policy responses. An econometric model is introduced that identifies factors which affect the likelihood of institution failure. Lastly, these factors are examined from the standpoint of determining FSLIC costs for a failed institution. The conclusions indicate that "the factors affecting the probability of failure may be different from the factors affecting the losses incurred by the FSLIC." Tables, charts, and references are included. This paper was also published by the Federal Home Loan Bank Board as Research Working Paper No. 117.

288. Barth, James R., et al. **Thrift-Institution Failures: Estimating the Regulator's Closure Rule.** Research Working Paper No. 125. Washington D.C.: Federal Home Loan Bank Board, January 1987. 34 p.

This paper presents an overview of thrift closures and previous studies of failures. A logit model is used to examine institution closure determinants. The model is based on the fact that closures are related to regulators' closure rules. Lastly, the authors evaluate the use of the model for predicting future closures. References are included. This paper is included in **Research in Financial Services: Private and Public Policy**, pp. 1-23, which is edited by George G. Kaufman. Mr. Kaufman's book was published in 1989 by JAI Press, Inc.

289. Benston, George J. **An Analysis of the Causes of Savings and Loan Association Failures.** Monograph Series in Finance and Economics 1985-4/5. New York: New York University, 1985. 182 p.

The paper was published by the Salomon Brothers Center for the Study of Financial Institutions at the Graduate School of Business Administration, New York University. The author examined statistically the financial statements of the 202 S&Ls that failed between 1-1-81 and 8-31-85. He concluded that the failures resulted from unbalanced portfolios due to long term mortgages being funded with short term deposits. He also analyzed the relationship between direct investments and the institution's financial strength. The author reviews studies of direct investments at S&Ls and comments on the results. He presents a risk analysis and states that no relationship between direct investments and failure is found. The regulatory restriction of growth and FSLIC risk is also discussed. Mr. Benston concludes with policy recommendations. References are included at the end of the book.

290. Benston, George J. and Mike Carhill. "FSLIC Forbearance and the Thrift Debacle." In **Credit Markets in Transition**, pp. 121-133. Chicago: Federal Reserve Bank of Chicago, 1992. 905 p. The 28th Annual Conference on Bank Structure and Competition, 1992.

The authors begin by pointing out that the 1992 Congressional Budget Office estimate of taxpayer cost for the failure of thrifts in the 1980s is $175-200 billion. They use a time series for the years 1979-1992, plus estimates of thrifts' current-value net worth to examine the role of forbearance in the loss. "Surprisingly, we find that forbearance did not contribute significantly, ex post, to the losses, and may even have saved money. This evidence is not generally consistent with the moral hazard hypothesis." The thrift failures in the first part of the 1980s bankrupted FSLIC but imposed "little or no acknowledged cost on the taxpayers." The 500 closures since 1984 account for most of the taxpayer losses. Benston and Carhill draw the following conclusions from their study, "It seems clear to us that the forbearance was not a major culprit in the taxpayer bill for the thrift crisis. Indeed, the largest portion of the cost is due to the 1979-82 interest-rate run up and the resulting insolvency at the majority of thrifts. Had these institutions been closed after they became interest-rate-risk insolvent, the cost of the funds disbursed to depositors would have had to have been incurred by taxpayers. In our view one lesson from the thrift debacle is most important. Financial intermediaries need much larger capital cushions against unforeseeable shocks." References are included.

291. Brewer, Elijah and Gillian Garcia. **A Discriminant Analysis of S&L Accounting Profits: 1976-1981**. Invited Research Working Paper No. 50. Washington, D.C.: Federal Home Loan Bank Board, September 1984. 63 p.

A survey of the S&L industry problems are presented by this paper which reviews data from 1976 and 1981. The characteristics of the strongest and weakest S&Ls are studied. A model is developed for examining the data. The study shows that the role relevant factors played was not constant over time. From this they determined that "caution should be used in extrapolating results . . . into other periods." Several tables relating to profitability are included. References are given.

292. Brumbaugh, Robert Dan Jr. **The Determinants of Failure and Insolvency for Federally Insured Thrift Institutions and the Determinants of Federal Savings and Loan Insurance Corporation Losses**. Ph. D. dissertation, George Washington University, 1986. Ann Arbor, MI: University Microfilms International, 1986. 193 p.

Mr. Brumbaugh is widely published on the thrift industry. His dissertation was directed by James Barth, also often published on industry topics. Both men were formerly employed by the FHLBB. An empirical evaluation of determinants of failure and insolvency are presented. Before 1980 examinations of the determinants of failure were also likely to be the determinants of insolvency because insolvent thrifts were closed by FSLIC. After that time, due to the large number of failures, "the determinants of failure is an examination of the insurer's reaction to insolvency but not necessarily an examination of the determinants of insolvency." The determinants of the insurer's costs are also examined. The paper begins with the history of the thrift industry. An overview of thrift failures from 1980-1984 is given; many tables are included. The effect of failures on risk taking is discussed. Significant regulatory changes from 1980-1985 are listed. A chapter is devoted to reviewing selected economic literature on thrift and bank failures. Authors included are Avery, Barth, Hanweck, Marting, Sauerhaft, and Wang. The remaining chapters of the paper discuss in detail the determinants mentioned above. The author suggests using estimated coefficients of the determinants of cost to develop the estimated cost to FSLIC for institution failures. He suggests using this information to structure a risk-sensitive premium or capital requirement which would be institution specific. Among the many tables included are FSLIC failures from 1934-1984; reproductions of FHLBB semi-annual and quarterly thrift financial reports; and the components of RAP net worth. A selected bibliography is incorporated.

293. Cates, David C. and Stanley C. Silverberg. **The Retail Insured Brokered Deposit: Risks and Benefits.** Washington, D.C.: Cates Consulting Analysts, May 1, 1991. 61 p. [65] p.

The role of brokered deposits in bank and thrift failures from 1987-1990 is analyzed by this report. The authors looked at the regulation of these deposits and at the brokered deposit business. They used data analysis of financial reports and interviews with brokers and bank/thrift issuers of brokered deposits. They reached five main conclusions which are covered in detail in the paper. The conclusions are: most failures have occurred in the absence of insured brokered deposits; other discretionary funding exceeded brokered deposits in failures; deposit issuance changed to sound issuers after FIRREA; the end investor is not wealthy; and retail insured brokered deposits offer balance sheet management to financial institutions at a cost lower than other funding. At the time of closing, only 34% of the failed institutions had brokered deposits; 82% of those had less than 5% of total deposits in brokered funds. The paper also points out that if the post-FIRREA brokered deposit restrictions had been in place in 1987, over 99% of the failed issuers would have had to secure regulatory waivers to continue issuance. Final conclusions are that since FIRREA, brokered deposits offer no greater risk to the insurance funds than other insured deposits. Also, no real benefits accrue to investors and issuers. The authors therefore assert that no benefit would result from withdrawing deposit insurance from brokered deposits. All of these topics are discussed in detail. A lengthy chapter deals with analysis of Lincoln Savings, Centrust Bank, and Franklin Savings' use of brokered deposits. Cates' "Thriftcompare" ratios, tables, and charts are included in this discussion. The conclusion is that there is no "compelling linkage" between brokered deposits and the failure of these three institutions. The appendix includes tables showing industry aggregates, incidence of failed and high risk issuers, deposit distribution, medians for high risk and failed issuers, and incidence of failed and high risk issuers by state and region.

294. Cole, Rebel A. **Insolvency Versus Closures: Why the Regulatory Delay in Closing Troubled Thrifts?** Financial Industry Studies Working Paper No. 2-90. Dallas, TX: Federal Reserve Bank of Dallas, July 1990. 41 p.

Evidence of "go-for-broke behavior by thrift owners" is revealed by the author's analysis. This paper examines insolvency and regulatory closure determinants in the thrift industry. The author points out that some thrifts studied were insolvent in every reporting period for ten years. The average GAAP insolvency before closure was 41 months for 800 institutions closed from 1980-1988. If supervisory mergers are excluded the average insolvency increases to 62 months. The author studies the differences in determinants of insolvency and closure. Thrift failure is modeled as a function of interest rate risk, credit risk, and principal-agent risk. References are given.

295. Cole, Rebel A., Joseph A. McKenzie, and Lawrence J. White. **The Causes and Costs of Thrift Institution Failures: A Structure-Behavior-Outcomes Approach.** Financial Industry Studies Working Paper No. 5-90. Dallas, TX: Federal Reserve Bank of Dallas, December 1990. 37 p.

The authors state that their study of moral-hazard behavior of thrift owners and managers differs from other studies "in that it employs a 'structure-behavior-outcomes' approach." A sample of 621 failed or failing thrifts with estimated cost of liquidation and 1,654 healthy thrifts was used. Portfolio decisions made in the mid-1980s influenced the outcomes in 1986-1989. These decisions were influenced by structural characteristics facing thrifts in the early 1980s. The model is presented, and the application and tests discussed. The authors state that "it appears that the proximate causes of the failures . . . of thrifts were . . . the new, nontraditional assets into which they expanded in the mid-1980s." Extensive references are included.

296. DeGennaro, Ramon P., Larry H. Lang, and James B. Thomson. **Troubled Savings and Loan Institutions: Voluntary Restructuring Under Insolvency.** Working Paper 9112. Cleveland: Federal Reserve Bank of Cleveland, September 1991. 30 p. [6] p.

Hoping that the thrift industry would recover, the regulatory agencies reduced capital requirements, did not enforce requirements, and allowed thrifts to hold more non-mortgage loans. This paper studies the largest 300 thrifts posting capital deficiencies at the end of 1979 to see if they used the flexibility to recover. Only 13% had recovered by the end of 1989, 55% had failed, and the remaining thrifts had less capital than in 1979. The paper reviews the differences between the insolvent thrifts that recovered and the ones that did not. Mr. DeGennaro used data from the FHLBB financial reports for 1979-1989. He found that most thrifts shifted away from traditional mortgage lending during this period. Only 13% of the thrifts survived and rebuilt their capital ratios to 5%. These thrifts held less risky portfolios than the non-survivors. Thus, the successful thrifts "pursued a different restructuring strategy than those that failed." The author notes that regulators would not have been able in 1979 to predict the survivors because there was little difference in the asset and liability structure of the 300 thrifts.

297. Elmer, Peter J. and David M. Borowski. **An Expert System Approach to Financial Analysis: The Case of S&L Bankruptcy.** Research Paper No. 144. Washington, D.C.: Federal Home Loan Bank Board, June 1988. 29 p.

An expert system is designed to analyze S&L financial health. It is modeled on the analysis of an experienced savings and loan analyst. The effectiveness of the system is evaluated. The results indicate that an expert system can be effective in predicting an institution's health. References are given.

298. Garcia, Gillian, and Michael Polakoff. "Does Capital Forbearance Pay and If So For Whom?" In **Merging Commercial and Investment Banking,** pp. 285-305. Chicago: Federal Reserve Bank of Chicago, [1988]. 630 p. Proceedings of the 23rd Annual Conference on Bank Structure and Competition, May 6-8, 1987.

The advantages and disadvantages of forbearance as a public policy is analyzed by the authors. The outcome of forbearance granted to thrifts from December 1982 - September 1986 is studied. Losers from forbearance are identified as: healthy thrifts paying higher assessments to fund the cleanup; non-thrift competitors; the supply of credit is reduced which decreases GNP; and "society loses from the inefficient allocation of resources." Stockholders, managers, and other "producers" benefit from the policy. This examination revealed that a number of thrifts did recover from 1982-1986, but the rate was low. Tables, charts, and references are included in the paper.

299. Kang, Heejoon. **A Dynamic Characterization of the Savings Institution Failure Determinants.** Bloomington, IN: Indiana University Graduate School of Business, October 1990. 73 p. [87] p.

The determinants and causes of S&L failures at specific times are studied using twelve accounting ratios. The results show significant differences in dynamic behavior between thrifts resolved in 1981-1983, 1984-1986, and 1987-1988. Results also showed significant discrepancies in the dynamic behavior of the twelve ratios for all institutions. The author states that the study suggests a need to construct a "series of lead-time-specific leading indicators" which would be updated frequently. Detailed information is provided on the construction of the accounting ratios and the thrift classifications. A statistical profile analysis is provided, and the appendices provide detailed descriptions of the data construction. References are included.

300. Kopcke, Richard W. "The Condition of Massachusetts Savings Banks and California Savings and Loan Associations." In **The Future of the Thrift Industry**, pp. 1-32. Conference Series No. 24. Boston: Federal Reserve Bank of Boston, [1982]. 187 p. Proceedings of a Conference held October 1981.

The past performance of Massachusetts mutual savings banks and California S&Ls are reviewed by this paper. These institutions comprise 19% of assets held by all domestic thrift institutions. The performance is reviewed using principles of current value reporting. The author states that "The results of the study suggest that the majority of thrifts will enter the 1980s in worse financial condition than their financial statements suggest." Further, two thirds of the thrifts may be insolvent by the 1990s, and unless capital standards are relaxed thrifts will not be able to grow until the 1990s. The study finds that the average CVR net worth-to-asset ratio for all thrifts is about -7%, and that an $80-$120 billion subsidy will be needed to raise the industry CVR net worth to 6%.

301. Moore, Robert R. **Brokered Deposits and Thrift Institutions**. Financial Industry Studies Working Paper No. 1-92. Dallas, TX: Federal Reserve Bank of Dallas, March 1992. 22 p.

Mr. Moore states that the findings from his study show "that concern about brokered deposits being used to exploit the shortcomings of the deposit insurance system is warranted." He uses a model which finds "a low ratio of capital-to-assets, high asset risk, low net income, and large thrift size are associated with intensive use of brokered deposits." The author points out that FIRREA and FDICIA attempt to curb use of brokered deposits. However, pricing deposit insurance to reflect risk would be a more direct approach. References are given.

302. **Report of the National Council of Savings Institutions Task Force on Operating Limits for Capital-Impaired Institutions.** Washington, D.C.: National Council of Savings Institutions, August 4, 1988. 5 p. [5] p.

The Task Force reviewed the growth of insolvent institutions and how it affects sound institutions and the FSLIC fund. It considered the need for additional restraints on insolvent institutions. The Task Force focused on the 444 insolvent and unprofitable FSLIC-insured institutions based on 1987 data. Four recommendations are made: insolvent institutions with no expectation of recovery should be prohibited from making new loans or acquiring new investments; supervision of these institutions should be shifted to a central unit at the Bank Board; restrict the growth at other impaired institutions; FSLIC-assisted acquisitions and mergers should be structured on a risk-averse basis.

Tables provided in the paper present data on growth at capital-impaired institutions.

303. **Report on Direct Investment Activities of FSLIC-Insured Institutions.** Washington, D.C.: Federal Home Loan Bank Board, February 10, 1989. 83 p.

CEBA required the Bank Board to examine direct investment activities. This report, a result of that requirement, was made to the Committee on Banking, Finance, and Urban Affairs and the Committee on Banking, Housing and Urban Affairs. The report analyzes the direct investment activities of FSLIC-insured institutions over various periods from 1983 through September 1988. The major components are real estate investments, service corporation investments, and equity securities. The report notes that the short period of time reviewed, and the economic climate affect the results. Most direct investments are long term investments. With this in mind, the results show that "most direct investments do not generate returns sufficient to cover the costs of funding them." Additionally the report shows: few thrifts are involved in direct investments; returns have deteriorated in recent years; thrifts most active in these investments have poorer returns than those with more modest levels of investments; and direct investments are only one factor in failures and "not an overriding one". Lastly, the report shows that thrifts that increased their direct investments after April 1987 have done relatively well. Many tables and charts are provided throughout the study.

304. Rudolph, Patricia M. **The Insolvent Thrifts of 1982: Where Are They Now?** n.p.: University of Alabama, [1989]. 15 p.

In 1982, 237 thrifts were GAAP insolvent. By 1987, 68 of the thrifts were GAAP solvent, with an average GAAP to total asset ratio of 5.6%. The author presents the factors which affect the probability of solvency. A logistic regression analysis is used for data for the period 1982-1987, internal and external sources of change in net worth are identified. Particular attention is paid to the raising of capital externally. The author states that "The issuance of new equity has a significant impact on the probability of insolvency in each year." She suggests that the process be simplified to allow thrifts to convert from mutual to stock institutions, so external capital can be raised. She points out that the variables differ widely in early years compared with later years. In 1982-1983 the asset composition of the thrift is important, in 1984-1987, credit quality is more important.

305. The Savings and Loan Crisis: The Dual System Unfairly Attacked.
Washington, D.C.: American Council of State Savings Supervisors, May 1991.
16 p.

This study compares state and federally chartered S&Ls during the 1980s.
Estimated resolution costs and number of resolutions are provided on a state by
state basis. A review of financial institution failures in Texas includes both
banks and S&Ls. It is noted that national banks failed at higher rates than state
chartered commercial banks in the 1980s in Texas. The study was undertaken
to dispel the belief that the crisis was caused primarily by state chartered
institutions. In only seven states did state resolution costs exceed federal costs
for S&Ls. Statistics are illustrated by charts and graphs.

306. Southern Finance Project. **Bailed Out Thrifts: A Profile of America's
Biggest S&L Failures.** Charlotte, NC: Southern Finance Project, 1990.
[75] p.

Selected financial information is examined for fifty-four of the largest failed
thrifts. Tables provide selected financial data, with emphasis on interest income
and deposits. The study shows that the institutions relied heavily on brokered
deposits, and invested extensively in junk bonds and other risky investments,
while investing less than the industry average in home mortgages. It also asserts
that these institutions contributed to the high cost of funds, and contributed to
lost tax revenues of more than $2 billion. Many tables and charts are used to
illustrate the findings.

307. Wallace, Nancy E. **Insolvency and Failure in the Savings and Loan
Industry.** Berkeley, CA: Institute of Business and Economic Research,
University of California, 1989. 38 p.

Ms. Wallace studies the portfolio management decisions made by S&Ls, and
how they relate to insolvency. An econometric model was developed to estimate
the probability of insolvency. A brief review of earlier studies of failure is
presented along with a strategy for estimating the model. Bibliographic
references are given.

TEXAS THRIFTS

308. **Bailed Out Lenders and Community Reinvestment: An Analysis of Mortgage Lending in Dallas, Houston, San Antonio, and Austin.** Charlotte, NC: Southern Finance Project, June 23, 1990. [27] p.

Mortgage credit patterns in Texas were surveyed for this study. Residential lending in 1989 by six large institutions created by the Southwest Plan and First Republic Bank bailouts were analyzed for four metropolitan areas. The study asserts that "at least 49 billion dollars" has been invested in Texas insolvent institutions, yet "virtually none of the money has been reinvested in minority neighborhoods in Texas' major cities." The study points out that only six-tenths of 1% of mortgage loans originated by these institutions went to nonwhite areas. Tables show mortgage loans by neighborhoods. It points out that the institutions were "skimpy investors in integrated neighborhoods", investing only 9% in these tracts. "A homeowner living in a predominantly white, medium income census tract in Dallas . . . was five [times] as likely to receive a loan from one of the lenders," the study argues. The institutions studied claim a significant portion of deposit marketshare. Tables show by institution a comparison of federal assistance and reinvestment, junk bond holdings compared to reinvestment, and deposit data. A detailed lender profile is included for each institution discussed. The institutions included in the study are: First Gibraltar Bank, Guaranty Federal Savings Bank, American Federal Bank, Franklin Federal Bancorp, United Savings of Texas, and NCNB Texas.

309. Born, Waldo L. and John A. Valenta. **A Synopsis of Texas Savings-and-Loan Associations' Operations.** Texas Real Estate Research Center Technical Report 286-1M-519. College Station, TX: Texas A&M University, [1986]. 38 p. [10] p.

FHLBB financial information indicated a major shift in the type of lending by S&Ls. A survey of Texas S&Ls was undertaken to identify the changes in lending operations that occurred during 1983-1984, and expected activity for 1985. The survey showed that significant changes in lending patterns had occurred. Significant increases were indicated in: whole loans and participations as percents of mortgage originations; proportions of loans originated for financing interim non-residential construction and land loans; proportion of all loans originated that were non-mortgage loans; and the proportion of total assets in non-performing assets. Significant decreases occurred in: proportion of total assets in federally insured loans, conventional loans, mortgage-backed securities, and fixed assets, and the percent of mortgage loans originated that were retained. The appendices include the survey, analysis, statistical techniques used, and a detailed analysis of each question. Also included is information on each saving association's lending and savings business generated at specific locations. The smaller association's lending was primarily in the home office area; the percent of loans made outside this area increased with the size of the institution. The authors note that, "The most surprising survey result is that associations made only modest changes in financial operations in response to regulatory changes."

310. Crockett, John and A. Thomas King. **The Contribution of New Asset Powers to S&L Earnings: A Comparison of Federal- and State-Chartered Associations in Texas.** Research Working Paper No. 110. Washington, D.C.: Federal Home Loan Bank Board, July 1982. 27 p.

The study was conducted because Congress was considering broadening the permissible assets for federal-chartered S&Ls. "Fortunately, Texas state-chartered S&Ls already have asset powers similar to those proposed in the Senate bills . . . ", state the authors. They compare the performance of state-chartered and federal-chartered S&Ls in Texas to draw conclusions regarding the possible effects of additional asset powers. Comparisons were made for the years 1977-1981. For these years institutions had a return on assets of 40 basis points while federal associations ROA was 33 basis points. The authors point out that evaluation of expanded powers must include how the powers affect exposure to interest-rate risk. Their conclusion is that "These powers permit asset diversification and better matching of the maturities of assets and liabilities, thereby reducing exposure to interest-rate risk."

311. Fabritius, M. Manfred and William Borges. **Saving the Savings and Loan: The U.S. Thrift Industry and the Texas Experience, 1950-1988.** N.Y.: Praeger, 1989. 161 p. index.

The chapters of this book follow the industry historically beginning with the emergence of S&Ls. Industry problems both nationally and in Texas are covered for the years of 1950-1965. The author characterizes 1979-1982 as the "First Crisis", and 1983-1988 as the "Second Crisis" in Texas and the U.S. The text shows how the Texas and national problems parallel one another. The "innovative reform demonstrated by Texas institutions" is reviewed. The author quotes Linton Bowmen, commissioner of the Texas Savings and Loan Department, as stating that "members of Congress copied policies . . . already established among Texas state-chartered S&Ls," when writing the Garn-St Germain Act. The final chapter summarizes the reform of the industry. This text provides a fairly detailed historical overview of the industry. Used in conjunction with the extensive notes and bibliography included, this source would meet the needs of those seeking only a review of the industry. For those requiring more detailed research this book should serve as one of the first references consulted.

312. **Governor's Task Force on the Savings and Loan Industry: Report to the Honorable William P. Clements, Jr., Governor of the State of Texas.** Austin, TX: Governor's Task Force on the Savings and Loan Industry, January 25, 1988. 57 p.

The task force was charged with obtaining a picture of the industry in the state, determining the state's responsibility, and offering suggestions to enhance state and federal cooperation. A review of the differences in asset quality between federal and state chartered institutions in the state is presented. The causes of the industry problems are examined and recommendations are given.

313. Horvitz, Paul M. "The Collapse of the Texas Thrift Industry: Causes of the Problem and Implications for Reform." In **Restructuring the American Financial System**, pp. 95-116. Edited by George G. Kaufman. Boston: Kluwer Academic Publishers, 1990. 180 p. index.

The macroeconomic explanations for recent financial failures are: high interest rates following the Federal Reserve operating procedures changes in 1979; inflation following the 1973 oil crunch; and the early 1980s deflation. The author points out that his focus is on thrifts, but "banks in Texas were inextricably tied in with the thrift debacle. Seven of the ten largest commercial banking organizations failed . . . Over 100 Texas banks failed during both 1988 and 1989." Mr. Horvitz discusses the effects of the decline in the oil, agricultural, and manufacturing markets in the state, as well as depressed real estate. He also discusses the structure of banking in the state, the impact of high interest rates, and the role of deposit insurance in the failure of Texas institutions. The FHLBB supervisory system as it existed in the early 1980s is explained; the lack of experience and adequate staffing is also discussed. This paper presents a fairly comprehensive discussion of all of the factors which contributed to the crisis in Texas. References are included.

314. Horvitz, Paul M. "Implications of the Texas Experience for Financial Regulation." In **Banking System Risk: Charting a New Course**, pp. 301-311. Chicago: Federal Reserve Bank of Chicago, 1989. 604 p. The 25th Annual Conference on Bank Structure and Competition, May 3-5, 1989.

The focus on Texas thrift insolvencies has obscured the fact that Texas banks are in a similar situation. The events leading to the thrifts' demise are unique and unlikely to occur again. The thrift and bank situations differed in that banks were not devastated by interest rate increases, so were not inclined to risk taking; bank examiners were quicker to spot problems and impose limits on risk taking; and FDIC addressed the problems quicker than FSLIC. The key element to reform is capital requirements. The regulatory agencies handled the problems very differently. The author notes that the FHLBB's Southwest Plan "was a reasonable approach to dealing with a very difficult problem. The Bank Board's major error in implementation of the Plan was in public relations." He notes that the traditional approach to dealing with failures would not have worked in the situation of dealing with over 100 insolvencies in the state of Texas. He also points out that the FDIC approach of whole bank transactions will not work for S&Ls in Texas. Several times the point is made that FSLIC's options were limited by the lack of cash to liquidate institutions. Lastly, the author cautions Congress regarding the actions needed to resolve the problems.

315. House Research Organization. **Tough Times for Texas S&Ls.** Special Legislative Report #140. Austin, TX: Texas House of Representatives, February 3, 1988. 23 p.

The financial condition of the Texas thrift industry is outlined in this report. The reasons for the problems are reviewed, and the impact on the Texas economy is examined. The Texas State Savings and Loan Department administrative authority and the Federal regulation of federally chartered institutions are described. The report identifies the major problems leading to the crisis as: overexpansion into new lending areas, especially commercial real estate development at the time the state's oil and agriculture economy started to crumble; loans to real estate developers for 100% of the appraised value; and including the first years interest payments as part of a real estate loan, even though thrifts received higher fees for larger loans this method of financing hid the weaknesses of the development. The report stated that "one out of every three problem thrifts in the country is located in Texas," and "more than one-third of Texas savings and loans were reported to have negative net worth on

September 30, 1987." Lastly the paper reports, "capital-to-assets ratio of Texas thrifts was minus 4.57 percent in September 1987." The impact of the Texas problems on other U.S. financial institutions was reflected as: pushing up deposit rates due to the "Texas Premium"; loan participations involving institutions in other states; and Texas loans packaged in mortgage-backed securities. The report also mentions the criminal investigations into land flips. Briefly described is the program developed for S&Ls across the country to purchase certificates of deposit at Texas S&Ls. Possible solutions under consideration and recommendations of the governor's Task Force are included. Selected references are given.

316. Perryman, M. Ray. **The Estimated Economic Impact of Excessive Construction Financing in the Savings and Loan Industry on the Economies of Texas and the Dallas/Ft. Worth Area.** Waco, TX: M. Ray Perryman Consultants, Inc., [1987]. 2 vols, various paging. A Study Submitted to the Dallas Morning News.

The degree of excessive lending by S&Ls in Texas was measured by this report. It also evaluated the impact of this activity on business conditions. The results indicated that between 1982-1986 approximately $2.4 billion in excessive real non-residential building activity was financed by Texas S&Ls. "This stimulus resulted in a total level of overspending in the economy of slightly more than $6 billion." Residential excessive building for the same years totaled about $8.8 billion and resulted in excessive spending of approximately $22.3 billion. The author predicts a five year recovery cycle. This study also includes analysis of the Dallas/Ft. Worth area. The two volumes which comprise this study easily contain over one thousand pages of data. Various aspects of the excessive activity are provided for each year studied with projections to 1990. Technical notes explaining the methodology are included.

317. Short, Genie D. and Jeffery W. Gunther. **The Texas Thrift Situation: Implications for the Texas Financial Industry.** Dallas, TX: Federal Reserve Bank of Dallas, September 1988. 11 p.

The interest rate premiums required to attract deposits to Texas institutions reflects the impaired confidence in Texas financial institutions. In 1988 Texas thrifts paid about 74 basis points above that paid by institutions outside the state. Texas banks paid an average 31 basis points. The authors state that banks and thrifts pay premiums for their deposits, and that the strongest institutions in the state are being adversely affected. Tables show the cost of deposits at thrifts and banks. The authors also explore the institution's asset quality problems. Tables present supporting data. The Southwest Plan is explained and analyzed. Short and Gunther explain that the thrift problem extends nationally. The purpose of this paper is to "highlight our concerns about the long-term impact of forbearance policies," the authors write.

318. Special Interim House Committee on Capital Formation. **Interim Report to the 70th Texas Legislature.** Austin, TX: House of Representatives, July 1, 1986. 87 p.

The subcommittee on regulatory activities sought to answer questions on several topics in this report. Among the topics covered are trends in federal regulatory activity, including the Federal Reserve, Comptroller of the Currency, FDIC, FHLBB, and the role the state should play in the decision process. A section is devoted to state authority over banks and non-bank financial services, and state regulatory authority. Trends identified as affecting institutions in Texas are oil prices, interest rates, and ATMs as they relate to capital formation in the state. Also discussed are state regulatory options which affect capital formation. A review is included of activities in other states and at the federal level which promote the formation of capital. The second report included is from the subcommittee on financial services. Provided are brief summaries of banking legislation from 1927 to 1982, and Texas branching and interstate banking laws. Structural changes in the Texas banking environment are discussed; this includes banks and S&Ls. Issues related to capital formation are examined. An appraisal of interstate banking proposals are given. Exhibits contain information by state on banking statues and inter-state banking.

319. **Texas Savings & Loan League Special Issues Commission: Report on the Texas Thrift and Real Estate Crises.** Austin, TX: Texas Savings & Loan League, October 30, 1987. 62 p.

The League created its commission when the Texas governor appointed a Task Force to study the S&L business in Texas. They studied the problems facing the industry, history of the situation, and possible solutions. The commission consisted of eighteen industry representatives and eleven non-industry representatives. The report states that the impact of the various historical factors led to increasing pressure on interest rate spreads and profit margins. These are problems which many thrifts sought to "grow out of". Seven problems are identified: cost of funds, net worth deficiencies, fraudulent and reckless activities, inadequate supervision and examination, disposition of troubled thrifts, and regulatory changes. Suggested solutions to the problems are presented.

320. **Texas Savings & Loans: Coming Out of Crisis.** n.p.: Hill and Knowlton, [1984]. 54 p.

The CEOs of 215 S&Ls in Texas were surveyed in June 1984. The objectives of the survey were to define the issues affecting the industry, to determine response to the deregulated environment, and to assess the strengths and weaknesses of the Texas S&L industry. The authors state that they feel the survey findings depict the concerns of CEOs and presidents at Texas institutions. They also state that the most important discovery of the study was the lack of emphasis on strategic differentiation. CEOs also indicated that planning was their most important issue after asset/liability management. However, the authors concluded from comments made that the institutions were generally in a reactive mode. There was also a strong indication that the respondents felt a need for a "moratorium on change" with comments that deregulation had left the industry in a weak position. Detailed responses to the survey questions are included.

321. **Texas Thrifts Impact of a Depressed Economy: Special Study.** Irving, TX: Ferguson & Company, May 1987. 22 p. [22] p.

A number of short term solutions to the S&L problems had been suggested, including the net realizable value concept, the deferral and amortization of loan losses, and relaxation of capital regulations. This consulting group advocated careful consideration of these suggestions due to the grave condition of Southwest thrifts. They focus on economic losses as opposed to accounting losses due to the dire economy in Texas. The study focuses on Texas thrift financial data as of 12-31-86. The institutions are divided into three groups based on financial health. Projections for one and five year periods are provided. The forecasts are dire for the state's industry. Detailed statistics are provided. The study notes, more than once, that early FSLIC assistance is needed to provide hope for a number of institutions. Suggestions and recommendations are made such as FSLIC recapitalization at the $15 billion level, development of an economic forecast for depressed areas for use in real estate evaluation, and amendment of loan classification regulations to more closely resemble those for banks. Twenty-two pages of tables are included which provide financial information to support the study results.

FINANCIAL INSTITUTIONS REFORM, RECOVERY, AND ENFORCEMENT ACT

322. **Analysis of Key Provisions of the Financial Institutions Reform, Recovery and Enforcement Act of 1989.** BNA's Banking Report Special Supplement. Washington, D.C.: Bureau of National Affairs, August 28, 1989. 21 p.

A short analysis of each section of FIRREA is given in this special supplement. It provides a middle ground between the very short descriptions of FIRREA, and the lengthy analysis available from other sources.

323. Barth, James R. and Philip R. Wiest. **Consolidation and Restructuring of the U.S. Thrift Industry Under the Financial Institutions Reform, Recovery, and Enforcement Act.** Research Paper No. 89-01. Washington, D.C.: Office of Thrift Supervision, October 1989. 29 p.

The major features of FIRREA are summarized in this report. Its consequences for the thrift industry are evaluated. Barth and Wiest point out that the industry will be safer and less of a threat to deposit insurance. However, restrictions placed on thrifts may impair their ability to diversify. Thrifts will become more specialized home mortgage lenders due to QTL tests and asset restrictions. Thrift charter advantages are reduced by FIRREA, and barriers between banks and thrifts have been removed.

324. Bloch, Stuart Marshall and Wesley S. Williams, Jr. **A Practical Guide to FIRREA.** New York: Executive Enterprises Publications Co., Inc., 1989. 869 p. index.

A glossary of "old and new acronyms" begins this FIRREA manual, which is followed by an index of key provisions. The authors, attorneys in Washington, D.C., provide background to certain provisions of the Act. They discuss the Bush administration's recommendations, the amended legislation approved by the Senate, the version approved by the House, and the final Conference Report. The first 362 pages of the book present the discussion of the Act. The Act itself is included in the following section of the book. The last part of the book contains statements by President Bush and Secretary Brady, fact sheets, and RTC initial releases.

325. Comizio, V. Gerard. "FIRREA: New Provisions Affect Structuring, Powers and Activities of Savings Associations." In **Raising Capital and Meeting the New Compliance Requirements Under FIRREA**, pp. [396-500]. [New York]: Executive Enterprises, 1989. [500] p.

Mr. Comizio was Assistant Deputy Chief Counsel with the Office of Thrift Supervision when this presentation was made. He examines many of the new provisions affecting S&Ls. Covered are capital standards, QTL test, exit and entrance fees, acquisitions, transactions with affiliates, holding companies, and activity restrictions. Regulations are referenced throughout the paper. Also discussed are junk-bond prohibitions, loans to one borrower limitations, brokered deposits, and loan limits. He points out significant changes as well as "little noticed provisions." This discussion is presented in a conversational manner.

326. Ely, Bert. "FIRREA: Implications for the U.S. Financial System." In **Game Plans for the '90s**, pp. 352-360. Chicago: Federal Reserve Bank of Chicago, 1990. 638 p. The 26th Annual Conference on Bank Structure and Competition, May 9-11, 1990.

Mr. Ely identifies three shortcomings of FIRREA: not enough money was provided to clean up the "mess"; an "unnecessarily complicated structure for the clean-up process" was created; and "it maintained a separate regulatory structure for the industry" which turned S&Ls "into clearly second-class citizens." Four problems which were not recognized when FIRREA was written have contributed to its flaws: overcapacity of deposit taking institutions; lost value of problem assets; government ownership of surplus decreases prices; and the massive quantity of problem assets RTC must sell. Mr. Ely predicts that "additional legislation is coming . . . I refer to it as Son of FIRREA." The new legislation will correct technical problems, reform deposit insurance, and modernize the banking structure. Issues related to deposit insurance reform are discussed. The author calls for a "100 percent cross guarantee concept."

327. Financial Institutions Reform, Recovery & Enforcement Act of 1989.
Chicago, IL: United States League of Savings Institutions, 1989. 10 vols. v.p.

The U.S. League published a group of booklets discussing various aspects of FIRREA. The booklets range from 10 to 34 pages in length. The League presents their interpretation of the Act and comments on the effect in these booklets: Capital Compliance, Conflicts of Interest, Corporate Restructuring, Enforcement, Financial Challenges, Investment Limitations, Legislative Overview, Operational Checklist, Real Estate Lending, and Regulatory Structure. The volume on "Financial Challenges" discusses the QTL test, state powers, equity investments, junk bonds, nonresidential real estate lending, and capital standards. The "Operational Checklist" provides the contents of the **Thrift Activities Handbook** and **Compliance Activities Handbook** using section numbers. Each topic in the checklist is identified as possibly having a substantial, moderate or minimal effect on S&L operations.

328. The Financial Institutions Reform, Recovery, and Enforcement Act of 1989: A Legal Discussion and Analysis of the Law and its Implications.
Washington, D.C.: Jones, Day, Reavis & Pogue, 1989. 467 p. index.

This publication is arranged in three parts. The first part presents an overview of the Act. A section-by-section summary of FIRREA comprises the second part of the book. The act is reproduced in the third section. The first section contains this short summary, "FIRREA constricts the range of permissible activities for savings associations, requires a significant increase in the Capital standards required of savings associations, imposes on these associations many of the regulatory restraints currently imposed on the banking community, and redirects the focus of the industry to residential finance."

329. "The Financial Institutions Reform, Recovery, and Enhancement Act of 1989 (S. 413)." **Bank Regulation & Legislation Review.** Washington, D.C.: Institute for Strategy Development, March 6, 1989. 54 p.

An analysis of FIRREA titles 2-11 is provided. A summary, impact, and analysis is presented for each title.

330. **FIRREA and Its Impact.** Austin, TX: Texas Savings and Loan League, 1989. [273] p.

Several topics related to FIRREA are covered by the papers which were presented at this seminar. A summary of FIRREA's key provisions are included in the first part of the manual. Joseph A. Muldoon presents "The Role of Savings Associations as Shareholders of the Federal Home Loan Banks after

FIRREA." The changes in the Bank System, its advances, and financial condition are addressed. "The Super Powers of the FDIC and Their Impact on Litigation and Contracts" is covered by Barry S. Zisman, this includes failed institution resolutions, special litigation powers, and the D'Oench doctrine. William Ferguson's presentation is "Thrift Survival in the New Environment." He discusses the new regulatory structure, the change in the Bank System, the state of the industry, and how to be a survivor. Ralph A. Mock reviews "Civil and Criminal Enforcement Actions and Penalties Under FIRREA."

331. FIRREA Handbook. Second edition. New Orleans, LA: Adams and Reese, 1989. 721 p. index.

A summary of FIRREA is presented first, with section references to specific items. The actual text of FIRREA follows and the technical amendments are included. A series of techniques are used to enhance the value of this text as follows: explanations are given in shaded boxes; new law is in regular text; and law that is amending or replacing prior law is in italicized text. Appendices contain the following information: schedule of effective dates; allocation of FSLIC regulations between FDIC and OTS; organizational charts, RTC interim conflict rules; and capital regulations issued November 6, 1989. Three supplements were issued in 1990. Supplement I covers "Strategic Plan for the Resolution Trust Corporation". Supplement II includes "OTS Fees, Conflict Rules, FDIC Insurance Study, Call Report." "Regulatory Organizational Charts, FDIC Appraisal Standards, FDIC Deposit Insurance Coverage" are discussed in the third supplement.

332. Gurwitz, Aaron S., Timothy Sears, and Michelle Deligiannis. **The Impact of the Thrift Resolution on the Fixed Income Markets.** n.p.: Goldman Sachs, May 1989. 31 p.

The probable impact of the FIRREA proposal on the Treasury and agency market, secondary mortgage market, high yield bond market, and money markets is described.

333. Heggestad, Arnold. "The Impact of the New Regulations on Thrift Operations and Profitability." In **Strategies for the Nineties,** pp. 77-99. San Francisco: Federal Home Loan Bank of San Francisco, [1990]. 197 p. Proceedings of the Fifteenth Annual Conference held December 14-15, 1989.

The S&L industry has been weakened by competition and other market forces. The author states that imposing conservative regulations on a weakened industry will reduce profitability to the point of eroding the number of institutions over the coming decade. Therefore, for most institutions the next decade will not be a period of growth. He argues that increased capital requirements "will prove almost impossible for a substantial portion of the industry." He also states that policymakers should remain consistent with their goals for the industry. Specifically they need to answer the question, "Is there a need for a thrift industry?" Mr. Haggestad comments on the major aspects of FIRREA and their effects on the industry. Issues discussed are reductions in investment alternatives, interest rate risk, accounting, capital requirements, and the qualified thrift lender test. Included in the proceedings are panel presentations on this topic by Russell Kettell, James Barth, and Roger Gordon.

334. Lofts, Robert L., Donald J. Querio, and Mark C. Jensen. **Financial Institution Receiverships Before and After the Financial Institutions Reform, Recovery and Enforcement Act of 1989.** [San Francisco: Severson & Werson], 1989. 87 p.

In addition to the numerous changes brought about by FIRREA, Congress also rewrote the receivership laws for financial institutions. The authors note that this law was stagnate because of its infrequent use between 1930-1980. This paper summarizes significant aspects of this law before and after FIRREA. The paper reviews the regulators and the insurance funds, pre & post FIRREA, and their functions. The paper points out that FDIC and FSLIC receiverships were not governed by the same laws. However, FIRREA gives FDIC and RTC the same powers. The appointment of receivers is covered under the old and new laws. Explanations are given for purchase and assumption agreements, conservatorships, MCP, and other transitional devices. Other major topics included are: jurisdiction of disputes, claims by the receiver against third parties, and treatment of creditor claims. Specific cases are cited and references to specific laws are made throughout. The authors conclude that there are still many problems to be cleared up by the wording of FIRREA, but that it is a "step in the right direction" toward clarifying receivership provisions.

335. Natter, Raymond. **Financial Institutions Reform, Recovery, and Enforcement Act of 1989: Pub. L. No. 101-72, 103 Stat. 183 (1989).** New York: Matthew Bender, 1989. 76 p.

A detailed explanation of the most significant aspects of FIRREA is contained in this pamphlet. Each title of the act and the important aspects of the title are covered.

336. **The New Financial Institutions Act.** [Dallas, TX]: Southern Methodist University School of Law, 1989. [619] p.

FIRREA is the subject of this program. As noted in the introduction "It is widely believed that FIRREA will speed the consolidation of the banking industry." A fairly comprehensive ninety-five page summary of FIRREA is included. In "FIRREA: Requiem for the Thrift Industry," Stephen Huber discusses housing finance as it existed as a social and economic arrangement. He states, "In social terms, thrift institutions were an enormous success. In economic terms, the . . . fortunate thing is that the United States was . . . almost free of inflation for so many years, else the thrift crisis would have come earlier." He continues by asserting, "It is time to put the thrift institution experiment behind us, and to design alternative strategies for providing adequate housing for all Americans." This manual includes reproductions of articles, **Congressional Record** excerpts, letters from the Justice Department, RTC fact sheets, and RTC news releases. Howard Feinstein, special counsel of the FHLBB, covers "Study Materials: Criminal Restitution and Criminal Provisions of FIRREA." Thomas Vartanian reviews RTC powers and responsibilities in his presentation. "Commentary on FIRREA: What Would George Bailey Think?" is the paper presented by Alvin Harrell.

337.   Pauley, Barbara.   **The Thrift Reform Program: Summary and Implications**. New York: Salomon Brothers, April 1989. 11 p.

A comment on the Bush administration's reform proposal (FIRREA), this paper gives financial figures for the plan and the budget impact. It reviews the regulatory reform, the issues likely to be controversial, and the impact on specific markets.

338.   Pauley, Barbara, Michael T. DeStefano and Bruce W. Harting. **The Financial Institutions Reform, Recovery and Enforcement Act of 1989: Overview and Market Implications**. New York: Salomon Brothers Research Department, September 1989. 18 p.

The financial structure of FIRREA is examined, including Refcorp and RTC. They quote two cost estimates, the first being $159 billion in fiscal years 1989-1999. A second, "broader measure" of $195 billion is given which includes additional elements, i.e. debt service for bonds and interest expense on Treasury debt issued to finance program costs. An overview of regulatory changes is included. The review of market implications covers mortgage-backed securities, the corporate bond market, equity and convertible securities markets, the real estate market, repo agreements, and swap, cap, and floor markets.

339.   Pulles, Gregory, Robert Whitlock, and James Hogg. **FIRREA: A Legislative History and Section-by-Section Analysis of the Financial**

Institutions Recovery, Reform and Enforcement Act. Colorado Springs, CO: Shepard's/McGraw-Hill, Inc., 1991. 2212 p. index.

Two volumes comprise this work. Each title and section of FIRREA contains the text of the new law. An analysis, legislative history, and reports are included for all titles, except Title I, for which an analysis is not given. The analysis portion of the text contains prior law, new law, "Senate Report--section-by-section analysis", and "House Report--section-by-section analysis". Explanations of House or Senate conference reports are sometimes given. The legislative history contains: President's Bill, Senate Bill, House Bill, references, index terms, and table of authorities. Conference committee information is included in some instances. The last part of the second volume includes "Prior Law" and several tables. Among the tables are abbreviations, glossary, FIRREA timetable, technical amendments, legislative amendments, significant colloquies, and significant floor statements. Tables of statutes and cases are also incorporated. A bibliography is given. This is a comprehensive guide to FIRREA.

340. Scott, Kenneth E. **Never Again: The Savings and Loan Bailout Bill.** Hoover Institution Essays in Public Policy No. 17. [Stanford, CA:] Stanford University, 1990. 24 p.

The author's "purpose of this analysis [is] to examine the adequacy of [FIRREA] to achieve its stated objective." The title of the paper is taken from Treasury Secretary Nicholas Brady's testimony on the legislation, "Two watchwords guided us as we prepared a plan to solve this problem-NEVER AGAIN." The causes of the collapse are examined beginning with the creation of the Federal Home Loan Bank Board in 1933. He notes that the specialization in mortgage financing with restriction on diversification automatically resulted in a maturity imbalance. Mr. Scott maintains that by the time Garn-St Germain was passed in 1982 to broaden investment powers it was too late to help. He examines the flaws in the deposit insurance system and the administration response to the S&L problems. The facets of FIRREA are probed. The author notes that the structural deficiencies of the S&L industry do not seem to be "sufficiently appreciated, and the incentive problem at the core of effective reform has not really been perceived and forcefully addressed." He continues his thoughts that "never again . . . may require more than a bit of good fortune." This essay has also been published in the proceedings of the 26th Annual Conference on Bank Structure and Competition by the Federal Reserve Bank of Chicago, 1990. It can also be found in **Restructuring the American Financial System**, edited by George Kaufman, 1990.

341. Shearson Lehman Hutton. **Impact of the Administration's Proposal on the Savings and Loan Industry: A Preliminary Analysis.** Washington, D.C.: Shearson Lehman Hutton, 1989. 12 p.

The Bush administration's proposal requires S&Ls to meet capital standards at least as stringent as those national banks must meet. Shearson Lehman Hutton developed a model to measure capital the institutions would be required to raise to determine the shortfall under these guidelines. Analysis was conducted under various scenarios with suggestions given for raising capital.

342. **Special Report on the 1989 Financial Institutions Reform, Recovery and Enforcement Act.** [Bethesda, MD]: Mortgage Commentary Publications, 1989. [69] p.

A discussion of FIRREA is presented in "every day" language. Each title is described. Comments are also included regarding various aspects of the Act.

343. **The Thrift Industry Restructured: The New Regulators and Opportunities for the Future.** Commercial Law and Practice Course Handbook Series No. 508. [New York]: Practising Law Institute, 1989. 630 p.

Mergers and acquisitions, stock conversions, and tax considerations are covered in this handbook. Two papers on FIRREA are especially useful. Cantwell F. Muckenfuss, III presents an extensive review of FIRREA. One section of the paper focuses on the agencies most significantly affected by the Act. The administrative transfer of FSLIC to FDIC and the resulting changes in regulatory, supervisory, and enforcement authority of the FDIC are covered. He also discusses the effects of the Act on the regulatory system for S&Ls, and the structure of the Federal Home Loan Bank System. The second part of his paper deals with the resolution of troubled institutions. The creation of the FSLIC resolution fund, RTC, and Resolution Funding Corporation are described. This is a very useful review of the Act. Thomas P. Vartanian's paper is a summary of selected provisions of the legislation which are significant to financial institutions and potential acquirers. He presents a brief synopsis of portions of the legislation, including: thrift activities, QTL test, RTC, S&L holding company provisions, and Federal Home Loan Bank System reforms.

POST FIRREA

344. Brumbaugh, R. Dan, Jr. and Robert E. Litan. "A Critique of the Financial Institutions Recovery, Reform and Enforcement Act (FIRREA) of 1989 and the Financial Strength of the Commercial Banks." In **The Reform of Federal Deposit Insurance: Disciplining the Government and Protecting Taxpayers**, pp. 117-143. Edited by James R. Barth and R. Dan Brumbaugh. [N.Y.]: HarperBusiness, 1992. 310 p. index.

A limitation of FIRREA is its exclusion of banks as a focus. The authors contend that the solvency of BIF would be of national concern if the attention were not focused on thrifts. They further argue that deposit insurance and the regulatory system have caused the deterioration of banks as well as thrifts. Although this paper's focus is the condition of the commercial banking industry, FIRREA is discussed. The critique of FIRREA covers its inadequacies in relationship to several issues. Covered in the discussion are regulatory reorganization, capital standards, asset restrictions, QTL test, and enforcement. The authors also discuss the lack of deposit insurance reform. Brumbaugh and Litan close by urging congressional evaluation of all the issues. In their words, "A sense of emergency seems in order." References are included.

345. **Consolidation, Liquidation, and Recapitalization: Banks and Thrifts Face the 90's.** Commercial Law and Practice Course Handbook Series No. 627. [New York]: Practising Law Institute, 1992. 1016 p.

This collection of papers is augmented by extensive reproductions of supporting documents in the appendices. A paper is presented on cross-industry acquisitions including an OTS memorandum on the "Super Oakar Amendment." Ross Delston discusses "New Regulatory Powers to Resolve Failing Banks and Thrifts." OTS materials are included for discussion. The materials relate to:

mutual holding companies, voluntary supervisory conversion regulation, FIRREA capital plans, prompt regulatory action, and voluntary unassisted transactions. Papers relating to RTC cover the issues of bidding, accelerated resolution program, and recapitalization.

346. Contracting, Litigating and Dealing With the RTC and FDIC. Englewood Cliffs, NJ: Prentice Hall Law & Business, 1991. 437 p.

Lawrence F. Bates' presentation, "Overview of Financial Institution Liquidations and Recent Legislation," discusses insolvencies prior to FIRREA. Included in this discussion is administrative receiverships, pre-FIRREA sources of law, and law applicable to assets held by FDIC and FSLIC in "corporate" capacities. BIF, SAIF, and the FSLIC resolution fund are covered in his discussion of the general structure of FDIC/RTC under FIRREA. He also touches on receivership appointments, liquidation provisions, and RTC/FDIC powers. This section includes copies of RTC news releases. Among other papers included in this text are "Conflicts Between FIRREA and the Bankruptcy Code" by William J. Perlstein and Russell J. Bruemmer, and "Negotiating Assisted Transactions" by Thomas Vartanian and Robert H. Ledig. Many articles on this topic are reproduced in this manual. The articles are taken from Bottomline, Banking Law Review, Banking Expansion Reporter, and Journal of RTC Real Estate.

347. Counselling Creditors of Banks and Thrifts: Dealing with the FDIC and RTC. Commercial Law and Practice Course Handbook Series No. 561. [New York]: Practising Law Institute, 1991. 719 p.

Lawrence Bates discusses "Bank and Thrift Liquidation Law and the Impact of FIRREA". Reproductions of RTC news releases, RTC statement of policy regarding treatment of collateralized letters of credit, and FDIC's Brief in Langley v FDIC are included. Recent developments related to net worth maintenance agreements are discussed by Michael E. Tucci. He also discusses recent bankruptcy code amendments. Rex R. Veal provides statutory analysis of contract repudiations under FIRREA. "How to Handle Real Estate Title Problems Created by Insolvent Depository Institutions" is presented by Janice E. Carpi. She covers options available to receivers and documentation necessary to insure title. Sample deed executions are shown. Another of the many papers included in this manual encompasses "Management and Liquidation of Failed Financial Institutions" by R. Neal Batson and others. This presentation examines interaction between government agencies, federal jurisdiction, and specific powers.

348. FDIC Improvement Act of 1991 and RTC Refinancing, Restructuring, and Improvement Act of 1991. New York: Matthew Bender, 1992. 65 p.

A synopsis of the two acts which are 1991's significant banking laws are provided in this booklet.

349. Gail, Daniel B., et al. **A Look at FIRREA to Date and An Overview of Strategies and Legal Issues Involving the RTC.** Eau Claire, WI: Professional Education Systems, Inc., 1990. [346] p.

This course book is divided into six sections. The first section, by Daniel Gail is, "A Compilation of Post-FIRREA Regulations, Guidelines and Interpretations." Among the items covered by Mr. Gail are: capital standards and capital issues, lending activities, dealing with failed and failing institutions, conversion, and RTC matters. "Practical Commercial Implications of FIRREA" is presented by Mark G. Magilow. This discussion includes lending limits and enforcement provisions of FIRREA. Superpower defenses and loopholes to the defenses are covered in "D'Oench, Duhme and Its Progeny Revisited" by Peter A. Franklin III. L. E. Creel III examines "Litigation Against the Resolution Trust Corporation." Presented in outline format the fifth section deals with "Negotiation and Litigation Strategy Under FIRREA From the Borrower's Perspective." Christopher M. Weil covers institution of the suit, jurisdiction, limitations, discovery, rights of RTC/FDIC, and forms of relief available. The last seminar presentation included in the notebook is by Robin I. Phelan and Donald C. Templin, entitled "'Dance With the One That Brung You' Unless it Was a Failed Savings and Loan Then You Have to do the Lambada With the Resolution Trust Corporation." This section covers litigation with the RTC, cost-effective collection of debts, witnesses and evidence, and litigation against the RTC.

350. **Impact of the Thrift Reform Act and the Future of the Thrift Industry.** Commercial Law and Practice Course Handbook Series No. 524. [New York]: Practising Law Institute, 1990. 800 p.

This manual begins with a list of 56 items related to a "Timetable for Implementation of FIRREA" by Cantwell Muckenfuss, III. Ninety plus pages are devoted to materials related to the RTC. The materials include reproductions of RTC and FDIC news releases, RTC organization charts, fact sheets, list of RTC institutions by state as of 8-9-89, and a buyers guide. Ronald S. Riggins paper, "Practical Guide to Capital Planning", includes TB 36 and TB 36-1. His outline of strategies includes moderate growth versus shrinkage, reduction of REOs, branch sales, and the sale/leaseback of a main office building. Thrift-to-bank charter conversions, structuring issues, and acquisitions of thrifts are covered in a paper by John A. Buchman. Thomas Vartanian covers "Thrift Capital in the 1990's: The Impact of FIRREA." He summarizes the current statutory and regulatory provisions and developments likely to have an impact on the amount and composition of thrift capital requirements. This presentation includes a list of "on-balance sheet assets assigned to various categories." Definitions of capital and "off-balance sheet items" are also discussed. Among the many additional topics covered are "The Acquisition Pricing of Healthy Savings Institutions" by Robert M. Adams, and "Tax Aspect of FIRREA" by Robert T. Cahill.

351. **Litigating For and Against the FDIC and the RTC.** Commercial Law and Practice Course Handbook Series No. 548. [New York]: Practising Law Institute, 1990. 400 p.

A few of the papers included in this handbook are: "FDIC Enforcement Actions: Rights Before Write-Offs," by Jeffrey C. Gerrish; "Discovery/FOIA Cases Involving the FDIC" by Charles L. Cope II; "Bank and Thrift Closing Challenges" by Thomas A. Schulz; and "Bank and Thrift Liquidation Provisions Under the Financial Institution's Reform, Recovery, and Enforcement Act of 1989" by Lawrence F. Bates.

352. **Litigating For and Against the FDIC and the RTC 1991.** Commercial Law and Practice Course Handbook Series No. 588. [New York]: Practising Law Institute, 1991. 768 p.

"Holding Company Liability for the Costs of Disposing of Failed Bank or Thrift Subsidiaries" by Howard N. Cayne, et al., is the first presentation in this handbook. It discusses "cross guarantee" provisions, net worth maintenance agreements, and "supervisory goodwill" cases. Exhibits included are briefs for Federal Reserve v. MCorp, et al., Carteret Saving Bank v. Office of Thrift Supervision, and Franklin Savings Association v. Office of Thrift Supervision. A paper by John G. Koeltl and Thomas N. Dahdouh, "Discovery from the FDIC", covers the special discovery problems for parties engaged in litigation with the FDIC. Another of the fourteen papers included is by G. Allen Carver, Jr., "The Financial Institutions Reform, Recovery, and Enforcement Act of 1989: Provisions of Interest to Federal Prosecutors". Rosemary Stewart discusses, "Criminal Liability for Pre-FIRREA White Collar Banking Related Offenses". She covers the status of defendants including: principle liability, secondary liability, aiders and abettors, and conspirators. Other aspects of her paper are misapplication or embezzlement of funds, false statements, false entries in books, bank fraud, and penalties.

353. **Litigating With the FDIC and RTC: Asset-Based Claims.** Commercial Law and Practice Course Handbook Series No. 559. [New York]: Practising Law Institute, 1990. 398 p.

Among the topics included in this handbook are: "Rights of Owners to Contest Actions Under FIRREA" by William J. Perlstein; "Contract Repudiation Under the Financial Institutions Reform, Recovery, and Enforcement Act of 1989" by Rex R. Veal; and also by Mr. Veal, "Dealing With the FDIC and the RTC: An Overview." Lawrence F. Bates' presentation "Bank and Thrift Liquidation Law, and the Impact of the Financial Institutions Reform, Recovery, and Enforcement Act of 1989" covers the structure of FDIC and RTC under FIRREA. Included is discussion on law applicable to RTC/FDIC liquidations, a general overview of liquidation provisions, and RTC/FDIC powers. Reproductions of RTC news releases, and FDIC's brief in Langley v. FDIC is included. T. Ray Guy covers "Unsecured Creditors." He comments on merits of claim, the "superpower" defenses of FDIC and RTC, and the collectability of claims.

354. Modernizing the Financial System: Recommendations for Safer, More Competitive Banks. Washington, D.C.: Department of the Treasury, February 1991. [631] p.

FIRREA directed the Treasury department to conduct this study. Proposals in the study include FDIC reforms, restoring competitiveness of the financial system, streamlining the regulatory system, and BIF recapitalization. Credit union reforms are suggested. Consolidation of regulatory agencies is suggested. The recommendations are included in 74 pages of the text. The remaining pages are "discussion chapters" which cover the history of deposit insurance, capital adequacy, scope and alternatives to deposit insurance, brokered deposits, risk-related premiums, accounting, interstate banking, FHLB System subsidies, and foreign deposit insurance systems. References are provided on many of these topics. This study brings together in one text a broad review of the industry which would be a good starting point for any research on the topic.

355. Representing Banking Institutions in the 1990's: Post FIRREA. [Dallas, TX]: Southern Methodist University School of Law, 1990. [662] p.

Extensive coverage of a variety of topics is found in this handbook. Included are speeches, papers, and reproductions of articles on related topics. Two papers by Rex Veal are included, "Contract Repudiation Under FIRREA," and "Dealing with the RTC: A Brief Overview." In "Professional Liability and Regulation of Financial Institutions" David Burns discusses negligence/malpractice and criminal and civil regulatory penalties which may be brought against accountants, attorneys, and appraisers. Daniel B. Gail covers "Thrift Capital Standards After FIRREA" in some detail. In his introduction he states, "If in retrospect it appears that linking tougher capital standards to more flexible investment policies would have helped to avoid the collapse of the thrift industry that does not mean that tying tougher standards to stricter investment policies will solve the problem or insure the survivability of the industry." He continues, "some observers argue . . . that FIRREA mandated capital rules coupled with its substantial reductions in thrift lending and investment limits is a primary cause of the continued failure of thrift institutions." He reviews core capital, tangible capital, and risk-based capital. The second section of his paper, "Enforcement Actions for Failure to Maintain Capital Standards", includes capital plans and limitation on asset growth. He also reviews three areas of relief from capital standards: capital exception, capital exemption, and limited growth. Extensive footnotes are provided.

356. **The Savings & Loan Crisis.** DPS Special Report-The S&L Crisis No. 31. [Washington, D.C.: Senate Democratic Policy Committee], August 8, 1990. 5 p.

A short overview of the S&L problems is presented in this paper. Resolution costs and numbers related to insolvent institutions are given. The new agencies created by FIRREA are outlined. Numbers are given for prosecution activity: RTC suspects fraud in 40% of thrift failures investigated; at end of February 1990 the U.S. Attorney's Office had 5,862 matters under review, with 1,489 cases pending; and in 1989 there were 2,336 cases of fraud filed. The S&L crime package the Senate passed as part of the Omnibus Crime bill on July 11, 1990, is described.

357. Shaw, Karen D., James C. Sivon, and Mary Johannes. **FIRREA: Implementation and Compliance.** Boston: Warren, Gorham & Lamont, Inc., 1991. 782 p. index.

The stated purpose of this manual is to "bridge [the] gap between the original law and the rules that will implement it" the understanding of which are "crucial to developing strategies that avoid regulatory pitfalls." Each chapter covers an area of law and discusses the regulations pertaining to it. The first chapter deals with the "new thrift industry," capital standards, and the RTC. The "Restructured Deposit Insurance System" encompasses BIF and SAIF, assessment schedules, conversions, exit and entrance fees, logo, FDIC, OTS, and the Federal Housing Finance Board. The RTC, its funding, obligations, authority, and duties is covered in the third chapter. Extensive coverage is given to the new capital standard, the QTL test, and asset and liability powers. The remaining chapters deal with holding companies, mergers and acquisitions, consumer and housing issues, enforcement division, and real estate appraisals. This comprehensive coverage is further enhanced by extensive appendices which include FIRREA (the Act), testimony, policies, forms, and instructions. A glossary is included.

358.   **Special Report on 1991 Bank Regulatory Reform Legislation.**
Bethesda, MD: Mortgage Commentary Publications, 1992. [75] p.

The Federal Deposit Insurance Corporation Improvement Act of 1991 was
passed in an effort to strengthen the banking industry. The legislation adds to
the regulatory burden of insured institutions, "probably will result in higher
deposit insurance premiums", and states that FDIC is the backup regulator for
banks and thrifts. This report discusses the various titles of the Act and
references section numbers. Specifically related to thrifts is the discussion on
QTL improvements, employee provisions, acquisition of insolvent S&Ls, early
intervention, thrift charter boost, CRA and HMDA provisions, OTS
assessments, and RTC issues.

359. Stanton, Thomas H. **A State of Risk: Will Government-Sponsored
Enterprises be the Next Financial Crisis?** n.p.: HarperBusiness, 1991.
225 p. index.

Focus on GSEs was instituted when a provision in FIRREA mandated a study
by the Treasury of government-sponsored enterprises, and the financial risk
which they pose. The purpose of the study was to avoid budget liabilities such
as those caused by the thrift crisis. The author was associate general counsel
at Fannie Mae in the early 1980s, and has worked with GSEs in many capacities
since that time. He contends that GSE accountability must be enhanced through
increased capital standards and improved financial supervision. The first chapter
deals with the thrift debacle. The similarities between thrifts and GSEs are
discussed. A review of various aspects of S&L failures precedes a discussion
of the financial and political parallels. The GSEs that relate specifically to
thrifts, Freddie Mac, Fannie Mae, and the Federal Home Loan Bank System are
discussed throughout the text. The various chapters deal with how GSEs work,
the "hidden cost", the market, politics, risk, accountability, and safety and
soundness. Tables and charts are found throughout. The author calls for
greater accountability for GSEs, he stresses the need to limit the risk as soon as
possible.

360. Stich, Michael J. **How to Profit from the Savings and Loan Crisis.**
Houston: Wilchester Pub. Co., 1989. 240 p. index.

A history of thrift institutions and regulatory agencies is presented. FSLIC and
FDIC policies for dealing with insolvent institutions are described. Mr. Stich
emphasizes the necessity of private industry becoming involved in the ownership
and management of foreclosed real estate and stresses the benefits of this
involvement. A bibliography is included.

361. Summary of Major Provisions of Banking Bill (S 543) from House Banking Committee: Federal Deposit Insurance Corporation Improvement Act of 1991. Washington, D.C.: Bureau of National Affairs, December 9, 1991. 47 p.

A short summary of each title and subtitle of this Act is given. The text of the "Conference Report on S. 543, Comprehensive Deposit Insurance Reform and Taxpayer Protection Act of 1991", as amended to insert the short title, "Federal Deposit Insurance Corporation Improvement Act of 1991", is included.

362. Understanding the Restructured Thrift Industry. New York: Law Journal Seminars-Press, 1990. 489 p.

Three major presentations compose this manual. "Major Statutory Provisions and Implementing Regulations Affecting Thrift Institutions Adopted After the Financial Institutions Reform, Recovery and Enforcement Act of 1989" is presented by Stephen M. Ege. As stated in the title this paper examines regulations which are intended to implement FIRREA. This is a lengthy discussion which includes insurance premiums, fees, growth, conversion between BIF and SAIF, QTL, loans to one borrower, capital, activities, affiliations, and regulatory structure. "Enforcement-Cases Involving the Office of Thrift Supervision" by Stanley M. Hecht contains memorandums, cease and desist orders, and notices of charges and hearings. These reproductions relate to Centrust Bank v. OTS, Charles Keating, Jr., Thomas Spiegel, and Thomas Spiegel v. Timothy Ryan, and United States Department of Treasury, and Office of Thrift Supervision. Julie L. Williams presents "The Post-FIRREA World for Thrifts: Developments in Mergers and Acquisitions and Challenges in Securities Disclosure Compliance." This section also consists of a series of reproductions. From **Banking & Financial Services** by Ms. Williams two articles on "The Savings and Loan Holding Company Act After FIRREA" are included. OTS orders related to voluntary supervisory conversions, TB 5a on capital maintenance agreements, TB 38-2 on capital adequacy, and TB 38-3 on voluntary unassisted transactions are included. Several **OTS Legal Alert Memo's** dealing with disclosures are provided. Also included is a **OTS Legal Guide** on the topic of "Management's Discussion and Analysis (MD&A) Disclosures by Savings Institutions" dated August 1989.

363. Wells, F. Jean. **The "Savings and Loan Cleanup": Federal Regulatory Arrangements and Proposals for Change.** CRS Report for Congress 91-810E. Washington, D.C.: Congressional Research Service, November 12, 1991. 11 p.

Proposals have been made which will affect the Resolution Trust Corporation and its handling of the thrift "clean up." The author first reviews the regulatory arrangements related to the clean up. The proposals for change which affect RTC and other government agencies are discussed. The proposals seek more efficiency and flexibility for the RTC. Recommendations for further reading are included.

SUBJECT INDEX

References are to entry numbers rather than page numbers.

AUTHOR INDEX

References are to page numbers.

About the Compiler

PAT L. TALLEY is supervisor of Library Services at the Federal Home Loan Bank of Dallas and the author of several articles.